The
Cambridge
Village

THE VILLAGES OF BRITAIN SERIES

Other counties in this series include:

Avon*
Bedfordshire*
Berkshire*
Buckinghamshire*
Dorset
Essex*
Gloucestershire*
Hampshire
Herefordshire*
Hertfordshire*
Kent
Leicestershire*
Middlesex*
Northamptonshire*

Nottinghamshire*
Oxfordshire
Powys Montgomery*
Shropshire*
Somerset*
Staffordshire*
Suffolk
Surrey
East Sussex
West Sussex
Warwickshire*
West Midlands*
Wiltshire
Worcestershire*

*Published in conjunction with
County Federations of Women's Institutes

The
Cambridgeshire
Village Book

Compiled by the Cambridgeshire
Federations of Women's Institutes from notes
and illustrations sent by Institutes in the County

Published jointly by
Countryside Books, Newbury
and the Cambridgeshire Federations
of Women's Institutes:

Cambridge
Isle of Ely
Huntingdon & Peterborough

First published 1989
© Cambridgeshire Federations of Women's Institutes 1989

Countryside Books
3 Catherine Road
Newbury, Berkshire

ISBN 1 85306 035 6

Produced through MRM Associates, Reading
Printed in England by J. W. Arrowsmith Ltd., Bristol

Foreword

Cambridgeshire is a county of waterways. Its rivers flow through chalk hills in the south and wooded claylands in the west to become the almost unique network of embanked rivers and large drainage channels of the now drained Fenland of the north-east of the county. Two cathedrals can be seen, one on the western edge of the Fenland at Peterborough and the other at Ely on the Isle of Ely often called 'The Ship of the Fens'.

The University City of Cambridge is well known, but the rural areas and their villages have many claims to historic interest and beauty.

The Prehistoric trade route, Icknield Way, runs along the chalk ridge in the south east, linking East Anglia and Central England. The Roman road, Via Devana, from Colchester through Cambridge links, at Godmanchester, with Ermine Street from Royston and becomes the Great North Road.

The WI Members and friends who have contributed to this book have enjoyed researching their village histories. There will be a warm welcome to all visitors from those who live in, and care for, these interesting and lovely villages.

Eileen Webster
Co-ordinator

Acknowledgements

The three Federations of Women's Institutes in Cambridgeshire have worked together to provide the material for this book. The Cambridge Federation, The Isle of Ely Federation and Huntingdon and Peterborough Federation would like to thank all their members and friends who have worked so hard collecting the information and drawings for this book. Also a special thank you to Eileen Webster who co-ordinated the whole project.

N

WISBECH

PETERBOROUGH
River Nene

RAMSEY

ELY

HUNTINGDON
River Ouse

Grafham
Water

CAMBRIDGE

River Cam

County of
CAMBRIDGESHIRE

Well Creek, Outwell

Abbotsley 🖋

Abbotsley is a fine example of an English village set in rolling acres of arable farmland, interspersed with coppices of mainly deciduous trees.

Its 13th century church stands at the highest point in the village, from which a wealth of old thatched or tiled cottages and more modern houses radiate outwards to the six farms forming the village boundaries.

Abbotsley boasts two public houses, both of which are focal points for villagers to gather and exchange views on village and national affairs and titbits of local gossip. The old Victorian school, which these days serves as the village hall, is in constant use for village activities.

The village's hand-carved wooden sign stands on the triangle of grass opposite the Eight Bells hostelry, and depicts the four stone figures on the church tower. Other attractions are the duck pond at the north end of the village, the children's playing field and cricket pitch on the south boundary and, of course, the village green, which is the site of the village fete and barbecue, celebrating the Patronal Festival each year.

If you walk through the village during the day, it is unlikely that you'd meet many people, other than the odd dog walker, but under this apparent somnolence exists a caring community, willing to share each other's joys, sorrows, defeats and triumphs.

The Abingtons 🖋

The Abingtons are pleasant villages about eight miles south east of Cambridge. Great and Little Abington are separated by the river Granta, but for social activities they are as one. The name Abington comes from an old Saxon name, Abba.

They each have a fine church dating from the 13th century, both in good condition. There is also a United Reformed church.

Mr Lewis, the schoolmaster until the Second World War encouraged cricket and rifle shooting in the village and these are still the village sports of today. His name is commemorated in a road name in the village of Great Abington. There is now a recreation ground where football is played and there are also children's play facilities.

Years ago ladies of the village provided a Parish Tea on Shrove Tuesday. This was followed by games and songs in the institute. Abington Fair was always held on the 29th of May and as the caravans arrived there was usually a thunderstorm! Mrs Emerson, of Abington Hall, came and paid for free rides for the children, and then the schoolchildren sang songs and received 6d. Peace celebrations in 1919, the coronations in 1911, 1937 and 1953, and the Queen's Silver Jubilee were remembered by events in the Cricket Meadow and other places.

The village institute was used during the Second World War as a YMCA canteen. Abington Hall was taken over by the army and there were many soldiers in camps all over the village. During this time a stick of bombs fell on the village, one being a direct hit on the bridge over the river. Great Abington church was damaged and consequently closed for repairs after the war.

In 1936 the government started the Land Settlement Association which bought land in Great Abington. Over 60 houses were built and each settler (many of them miners and families from South Wales and the North East) had a plot of land to cultivate. Pigs and chickens were reared and various arable crops grown. Now large quantities of tomatoes and salad crops are grown in the 60 ft. greenhouses. After the government gave up the scheme, many plots were sold to individual settlers.

Not many inhabitants work on the farms in the area as in past days. Now, many commute to work in Cambridge, Haverhill, Saffron Walden and even London.

The British Welding Institute bought Abington Hall after the war and now employs hundreds of people from many miles around. Very important and highly technical work is done there.

Many new estates have been built in the past few years, Magna Close, Lewis Crescent and Close, and Mortlock Gardens in Great Abington and Westfield in Little Abington, and all who live here now, are taking a keen and helpful interest in village affairs.

Alconbury & Alconbury Weston

The Alconburys are situated north west of Huntingdon. These two attractive villages are surrounded by arable farmland. Although physically one mile separates the two villages both communities participate in the various activities and services.

The name Alconbury has become well-known around the country thanks to the air base here shared by the RAF and American Air Force. Surprisingly, there is not too much noise from the air traffic and the villages have become increasingly popular with housebuyers over the past few years.

But there are many more interesting points to the twin villages of Alconbury and Alconbury Weston, including the many fords and bridges which cross Alconbury Brook as it winds its way through the countryside.

In particular, there are two historic bridges worthy of note. Both are built of ashlar, square hewn blocks of stone and Alconbury Weston bridge incorporates materials alleged to have come from Coppingford church. Described as a medieval platform bridge, it consists of a central pier and two abutments of ashlar with a modern timber structure.

Alconbury bridge, not far from the parish church, has been repaired in recent times with brick parapets, but is believed to date from the 15th century. The interesting design comprises four spans with segmental-pointed arches, chamfered on the face and with cut-water piers. The easternmost arch has been re-built and is semi-circular; other similar repairs have also been carried out.

Although the village is close to the A1, and therefore ideal for rapid cross-country communications, residents enjoy a natural rural environment. The green forms an attractive central feature, the brook passing through is often lively with ducks and geese.

The Alconburys share the fine 13th century church of St Peter and St Paul. The west tower has a broach spire and inside are fragments of wall paintings and medieval glass. The church is a very beautiful building and has been a witness to the Christian faith for over 700 years!

The modern Alconburys have a population of around 2000, just over a quarter being Americans from the nearby airbase. Formerly this was an RAF base, built in 1938, but it is now run by the American air force. It is a source of local employment in the area, though many commute to other areas.

The villages have good facilities including a junior school, pubs, shops, post offices, C of E and Methodist churches and a surgery with pharmacy and a community nurse.

Alwalton 🦢

Situated five miles south west of the expanding cathedral city of Peterborough, this conservation village is bounded to the west by the A1 (London) road, to the south by the A605 Oundle road and to the north by the Nene valley, which provides attractive walks either across the valley to Castor or through Lynchwood to Ferry Meadow, an extensive country park.

Through the valley, from Wansford to Peterborough, runs the Nene Valley Steam Railway, a popular summer attraction.

Alwalton is the home of the East of England Agricultural Society which, each July, stages one of the most prestigious agricultural shows in the country. It also hosts the National Shire Horse Society Show in March, the Ponies of Britain Show in August, Expo-Steam and numerous other events.

The focal point of this village is its fine Norman church of St Andrew, started in the 12th century and extensively restored between 1961–1966 by the beneficence of Canon The Rev. Dr Grimes DD (a former civil engineer), the then parish priest. The other notable buildings are Georgian Alwalton Hall, the Jacobean Manor Farm and the Old Rectory. In addition there are numerous old cottages, some thatched.

The old Victorian School opened in 1846, but through falling rolls closed in 1981 eventually being acquired by a local chartered civil engineer, who whilst preserving all its original features sympathetically converted it for professional office use.

The local hostelry, the Wheatsheaf Inn is another old building, and close by is the tiny post office/village store and the old blacksmith's (now a private house). The village hall was erected to the memory of Colonel Dane, who formerly resided in Alwalton Hall.

The village was the birthplace of the famous Frederick Henry Royce, born 27th March 1863, the youngest of the five children of James and Mary Royce. He lived here for only the first four years of his life, moving with his father to London, but returned to Peterborough aged 14 to take up an apprenticeship at the Great Northern Railway Works. He subsequently became an electrical engineer, with a partner forming F.H. Royce & Co in 1884. After some years of struggle he built the first Royce 10 horse power car in 1903/1904, before becoming co-founder of Rolls Royce. There is a plaque to his memory in St Andrew's church.

Another notable resident for a time, to whom there is also a plaque in St Andrew's church, was Francis Arthur Perkins, the founder of Perkins Engines, world famous for its diesel engines. He lived in the Hall prior to his death on 15th October 1967 and he and his wife are interred in St Andrew's churchyard.

Babraham

Babraham was one of the important ancient settlements in this part of the county, situated as it is at the foot of those important defence posts the Gog Magog hills. Two very ancient highways run by it; the Icknield Way, a prehistoric trade route which runs by Bourn Bridge, and Via Devana, the old 'Worsted Road' which runs along the Worsted Dyke by the northern edge of the settlement. It is thought too that the street which runs past the Madeline Hill across the main road and through the chalky hill to Worsted Lodge is very old.

In 1575 Babraham was owned by Robert Taylor who built himself a very fine house in almost the same position as the present hall. This was described as one of the first Gothic houses in the country. In 1593 Horatio Palavicini, a Genoese adventurer became the owner. He was a political agent for Mary Tudor and after her death changed his religion and became moneylender to Elizabeth I. He commanded an English man-of-war during the Armada.

Babraham Hall was built by the Adeane family in 1833–37. It replaced at least three other houses which have stood on this site. They remained here until the house was sold to the Agricultural Research Council in 1948, although they still owned most of the land in the village which was subsequently sold on the death of Sir Robert Adeane. His daughter and grandson still have houses in the village.

In the Middle Ages the village was wealthy, being assessed higher than any other village in Chilford Hundred excepting Linton. Babraham had an open field system with fields varying in number from four to six. The open fields were enclosed during the period 1794–1829 without a formal agreement as almost all the land was in the possession of the owner. This fact has enabled more advanced methods of farming to be employed here than elsewhere. Most important was the breeding of both sheep and cattle by Jonas Webb, tenant of Church Farm. He acquired a worldwide reputation for his achievements. A statue of him bought by subscription from his 'Friends in Many Lands' stands in the village street, this formerly stood in the Corn Exchange in Cambridge.

The church dedicated to St Peter is a very fine building with an impressive tower which is the earliest part of the building dating from the 12th century. The remainder of the building as it stands, dates from the 13th and 15th centuries. The chancel dates from mid 13th century and nave and aisles from the 15th. There were at one time five bells but only one now remains.

In the centre of the village opposite the George Inn are a row of almshouses with the old schoolhouse in the middle. The school was established under the will of Judith Benet though there had been a schoolmaster in the village as early as 1607. The school provided free education for the children of the village and was in use as a primary school until a new one was built in 1959. This new school is opposite the vicarage.

Next to the George Inn on one side stands the oldest house in the village, Chalk Farmhouse. On the other side is a row of Victorian farmworkers' cottages, now much improved from the days when the tenants had to fetch their water from a pump outside the George Inn.

Balsham

The village of Balsham, in the very south east corner of Cambridgeshire, is an old (pre Domesday) and thriving village, originally agricultural and completely self-sufficient. The village has changed with population trends, dropping in numbers as agriculture dwindled and people moved out of the countryside to the cities but now doubled again in size to last century's level of about 1500 people and 500 houses. It is due to expand further with the latest County Structure Plan.

Electricity did not reach here until 1949 and sewerage not for another 14 years, and still there is no gas. Balsham is classed as a larger village, having the local junior school, post office, butcher, stores, builder and builder's merchant, agricultural merchant and dairy with local deliveries. There are many small established businesses run from the village.

Balsham is an active community and one of its more unusual events is the Plough Monday celebration. On the second Monday in the New Year a dozen or so old ploughmen (or similar nowadays!) haul a hand plough around the houses and pubs (three) collecting for a local charity. Those who do not contribute traditionally have their lawns ploughed through! Another popular event is the 'Mile of Pennies', organized by the cubs and scouts who lay out a long line of 2p pieces one Saturday morning from the bottom pub up to the top pub. Donations are collected from every passer-by (whether he's already been caught or not).

There are still many old and worthy properties in the village, a lot of them thatched, and there are 36 Grade II listed buildings.

The church of Holy Trinity is said to have been defended by Balsham's last survivor against the Danish hordes in the early 11th century, a heroic feat commemorated in the village sign. The centre of the village is now being designated a conservation area.

Bar Hill

Bar Hill, a new village created in the middle of farmland, came into being at the suggestion of the Cambridgeshire County Council, as an alternative to ribbon development. It lies seven miles to the north west of Cambridge, just off the old Roman road of Via Devana now known as the A604.

The first intimation of a new parish came to the inhabitants of Dry Drayton in 1948. It was given ministerial approval in 1964 and 350 acres of land in the parish of Dry Drayton were acquired. There was opposition to the plan, including some from the nearby National Institute of Agricultural Botany, who feared that pollen from gardens would seriously affect their experiments, hence the original ban on growing any member of the cruciferous group of plants. The ground had previously grown fruit for a jam factory at Histon.

The new parish was planned around a large village green, with school, village hall and church bordering on it. An area apart from these was set aside for industrial development and shops. The Radburn Principle developed by Clarence Stein and Henry Wright at Radburn, New Jersey was adopted and pedestrian and vehicular traffic are separated as much as possible. A road encircles the village with a number of cul-de-sacs leading to the centre, so that the main facilities are within easy walking distance of all parts of the village. This also allows for small communities within the main residential part with safe areas for children to play. Unfortunately, not all the excellent facilities planned were carried out. At first the project did not succeed, but a few hardy pioneers persisted and now it has become a success story.

The village has adopted as its logo the great bustard, a bird which formerly lived here but is now extinct in this country.

Before the Dissolution of the Monasteries the land belonged to Crowland or Croyland Abbey in Lincolnshire. The abbot had authority to hang thieves caught red-handed. At least 12 skeletons were discovered at Galles Piece near the Dry Drayton/Oakington crossroads during roadworks. One abbot is said to have hanged a man for stealing 16 eggs, although this was not on his land.

Another discovery was a Saxon drinking vessel which is now in the Fitzwilliam Museum in Cambridge. For a period the land belonged to the Cutts family who lived at Childerley or Cildersley, later it was bought by the Duke of Bedford whose main purpose was to create a park. Some of the old field names are retained. Thruffles is a corruption of 'three furrows', so called because the nature of the ground made it necessary to plough it three different ways.

Barnack 🌿

Barnack has been described as a village that has 'grown from its own earth'. Almost the entire village is built on land from which stone was quarried from Roman times to the 16th century, and the 'ragstone' has been used for important buildings throughout East Anglia, including the abbeys of Crowland, Ramsey and Bury St Edmunds and Peterborough and Ely cathedrals.

The village lies just off the Roman Ermine Street and the first mentioned record of Barnack is in the Anglo Saxon Chronicle of the 9th century where it is spelled Beonica.

The church which is built of Barnack ragstone is of great interest. Some of its notable features include the Saxon tower dating from 1020 with a broach spire added around 1200. In the north aisle there is a perfectly preserved 10th century Anglo Saxon sculpture of Christ in Majesty and a fine 13th century font.

In 1976 a National Nature Reserve was created on the 22

Kingsley House at Barnack

A. Storm

hectares of the old quarry workings. These hummocky spoil tips, known as the 'Hills and Holes' contain a variety of rare plants characteristic of limestone soils. Barnack is one of the two richest sites in Britain for the beautiful pasque flower and the grasslands also support a wealth of vetches, cowslips and rare orchids.

In 1965 a new estate built on the former parkland of Kingsley House won a Civic Trust Award for its successful blending into the heart of the village.

In 1796 the stone building situated in School Lane, was built by the 1st Marquis of Exeter for 140 children. It was leased to the National Society for the Education of the Poor. A new infant room was added by the rector in 1896. This stone building is now Barnack village hall known as the Wilfrid Wood Hall. The present school was officially opened in 1951.

Among many old and interesting buildings in the parish are two houses of special interest. One is the former rectory built in the 14th century and now known as Kingsley House. It was here that Charles Kingsley, the novelist, spent his childhood during his father's ministry. The second house, standing two miles from the village, is Burghley House. William Cecil, later Lord Burghley

17

(Lord Treasurer to Queen Elizabeth 1) acquired the manor of Barnack and built the magnificent palace in the latter half of the 16th century. Burghley House is still occupied by the Cecil family.

Barrington 🌿

Barrington is situated eight miles south of Cambridge, with a population of about 1000. The village is most attractive with its large expanse of green consisting of some 23 acres and the mile long street running through the centre. Both old thatched cottages and new houses blend together around the edge of the green. Many years ago villagers who owned cows and horses would pay ten shillings per year for grazing rights, whereas goats and geese could graze free of charge. Some feel it is a pity this no longer takes place, as the cattle seemed to give added charm to the village scene.

The church is dedicated to All Saints, under which name it is mentioned in 1400. The church is quite big and is said to have been built with the chalk from the local pit on the outskirts of the village. Barrington is dominated by two tall chimneys puffing their white smoke across the sky. They belong to Rugby Portland Cement Company and cement has been produced there since 1900. The cement is despatched by road or by a light railway that is linked to the main line at Foxton. Many years ago when boys left school they either went into the cement factory or on the farms to work as there was so little choice. Arable farming goes on today, but there are no dairy farms now.

The Church of England primary school and schoolhouse were built in 1838 and the roofs are thatched in Tudor style. A tradition of the school was to celebrate May Day each year with dancing around the Maypole either in the school playground or on the village green. A May Queen and her attendants would be chosen, and the boys would carry staves decorated with flowers while the girls would carry garlands, all made at home with help from their mothers. Prizes would be awarded for the best display. This tradition was discontinued in the 1960s.

The windmill standing south of the green was also built with clunch in 1822 and stood derelict for many years until it was renovated and converted into a modern home (minus sails of course).

The river Rhee flows through the parish and in medieval days was said to be the boundary between Mercia and East Anglia. Bulbeck Mill stands along the river bank and acquired the name in about the year 1240. It is no longer a working mill but thrives as the Barrington factory of Grant Instruments, makers of scientific instruments.

A character often remembered by older parishioners was Fred Patman. On Rogation Sunday he would don top hat and tails, and complete with handbell and sword would 'Beat the Bounds' and walk along the Roman Road to the 'Old Guildhall'.

Barton

Barton is a village of approximately 950 inhabitants situated three miles south west of the university city of Cambridge. It was a flourishing village in Saxon times and is mentioned in the Domesday Book. Roman remains have been found within the village boundary including slave chains and the fire-dogs which are now housed in the Cambridge Museum of Archaeology.

St Peter's church dates back to the 12th century but the style of the present church is pure 14th century. It was probably at the time of William Dowsing that the wall paintings, which since 1320 had covered the entire walls of the nave, were concealed under whitewash. In 1929 they were restored to view, and in 1980 a five-year programme of conservation was introduced. The 14th century screen and the pulpit bearing the date 1635 are much admired. The church has five bells.

There are two public houses, The Hoops and The White Horse. The latter used to brew its own beer on the premises. When it was kept by three elderly ladies, they displayed a sign 'No Swearing'.

An annual event in the the past was the Village Feast with stalls in School Lane and Hoops yard. There is now a Horticultural Show in July when many of the village groups are involved.

There are tales of a village ghost which frequented one of the farms. An account of these happenings is told in the song *The Knocking Ghost of Barton*.

The recreation ground has a bowling green and a hard tennis court, and also swings and a see-saw for the children's corner. The village has a football team and in years past there was a cricket team and tug-of-war team. Alongside the recreation ground there is a strip of grassland about one quarter of a mile long, known as

The Leys, pronounced 'lays' which, over the years, has become common ground. In years past it was used as an archery ground.

Situated on the outskirts of Barton is the Mullard Radio Astronomy Observatory. The Cambridge University radio telescopes have been built along the line of the old Cambridge to Bedford railway.

The Ministry of Defence Rifle Range is situated on the outskirts of the village and nearby are the kennels of the Trinity Foot Beagles.

Bassingbourn-cum-Kneesworth

Bassingbourn is an Anglo Saxon name and the first settlement was probably in the Bowling Alley area, which is situated beside the brook.

John of Gaunt owned a castle at the north end of the village – a public house near the site of the castle was named after him. Years ago it was converted into a private house, and still has the same name. It is reported that Oliver Cromwell's mother resided in the house known as Church Farm.

The parish church, St Peter and St Paul, situated in North End was built in 1272. The chancel was erected in the middle of the 14th century. The Congregational church which is in the recreation ground, (formerly known as Meeting Close) was built in 1791. In 1982 the church was condemned as unsafe, and services are now held in a small building in South End.

In 1840 the notorious case of the unburied child commenced. The infant Jane Rumbold, born the 12 December 1839, was baptised by the non-conformist minister, C. Moase on 8th February 1840 and died on 14th February 1840. Application was made to the vicar Reverend W. H. Chapman for interment in the churchyard; the vicar refused to bury the child – he said he would not bury any child that was baptised at the Meeting. Five times the body of Jane Rumbold was taken to the churchyard. Eventually a judge at a High Court declared the baptism valid, and the vicar lost the case after five years' litigation. The child had been kept in the house, a recess being made in an empty chimney to preserve the body – the corpse had been taken to and from church so many times that a second coffin had to be made. The vicar still would not perform the service, but the vicar of Whaddon, the Reverend W. Coulcher buried the child on 30th January 1845. On a bitterly cold, wintry day, snow fell fast. Notwithstanding, the people turned out in crowds to hear the bell tolled and to witness the burial of the child by the side of her mother and ten of her brothers and sisters in the Parish churchyard.

About 1850 a Cambridge professor discovered coprolites here. The excavation of these fossil phosphates provided a prosperous industry over the latter half of the century during which time the population almost doubled; much labour was imported and this led to vagrancy in the locality. Coprolites were dug by hand, washed, loaded and carted to Royston station.

Straw plaiting, a part-time industry, was carried on by women in their houses – this found favour for a considerable time. The straw plait was sewn onto bonnets and hats modelled on stone moulds. Some of these moulds are still in the village.

In the first decade of this century there were about 1,200 inhabitants, now there are 3,500. At one time there were 14 shops in Bassingbourn and one in Kneesworth. There are now six shops in Bassingbourn and one in Kneesworth. There were 12 public houses in Bassingbourn and two in Kneesworth. There are now two in each location.

A famous inhabitant lived at Kneesworth Hall in the early part of this century. He was Lord Knutsford, the second Viscount. Before he succeeded to the title he was the Honourable Sydney Holland. At this time he was appointed Chairman of the London Hospital in Whitechapel, where some of the wards are named The Holland Wards. Not only in London but in Bassingbourn and Kneesworth he showed his care for others. He saw the need for a District Nurse, and brought one from the London Hospital and paid her from his own pocket. When village people needed urgent hospital treatment he arranged for them to be admitted to The London and paid their fare, or took them in his own carriage. He built and equipped a village hall in Kneesworth and was a member of the local cricket club. When Sir Peter Scott was a small boy he spent long periods at Kneesworth Hall as Lord Knutsford was his guardian.

In 1936 the Air Ministry acquired nearly 500 acres of arable land in Bassingbourn and Wendy for the erection of an aerodrome. This provided employment of all kinds for many people in the locality. During the Second World War it was a Bomber Station and many bombing raids were carried out over enemy targets by pilots stationed there. The base is now a barracks for training soldiers.

Benwick 🦢

Benwick is a unique fen village, being built on a rodden, but drainage has caused the peat to shrink and the rodden to be lowered, and this has caused buildings to tip and crack, until, in the past, they finally either fell down or were pulled down.

This means there are few really old buildings standing, the main one remaining being the village school which was built in 1873.

The Wesleyan chapel built in 1833 does still stand, although the walls and floors are tilting. The Baptist chapel built in 1818 was pulled down in the 1960s, and St Mary's church built in 1850 was pulled down in 1985. However, other churches received some benefit from this, as stained glass windows went to Doddington church, the font and the door to St Jude's church in Peterborough, and the clock was sent to March Museum.

Once all the inhabitants (apart from the schoolmaster, the rector, the village policeman and the sub-postmaster) earned their living from the land. In 1899 it was noted that a boy was absent from school for 'cow-tending', and children were continually absent to work on the land at potato-picking time and gleaning. It seems that the only fun they had was to take time off for a Band of Hope

Benwick village

Demonstration or picnics and Sunday School festivals, for Plough Monday or the Village Feast in July, and they were late for school on May Ist 'through being out with garlands'!

There were seven public houses in the High Street, but now only one remains, namely The Five Alls, standing for 'I govern all, (the Queen), I plea for all (lawyer), I pray for all (parson), I fight for all (soldier) and I pay for all (working man)'.

During the Second World War there was a dummy areodrome in the village, which used to trick enemy aircraft into thinking they were over an RAF camp or the marshalling yards at March. More bombs dropped at Benwick than anywhere else in the county, sending London evacuees scuttling home because they felt safer there!

It is true that the face of Benwick is changing. The damp, low cottages are being replaced with smart, centrally-heated homes. When asked why they choose to move to Benwick newcomers answer that it is for the peace and quiet, and that once they see the sign 'Benwick', they know they are out of the rat-race once more.

Bluntisham 🌿

Bluntisham is situated four miles east of St Ives. It was part of the old county of Huntingdonshire. This village has a very long history. The prehistoric occupation of this area is suggested by the discovery of flint tools. Romans too, used this site, leaving pottery vessels and a bronze statue (now housed in the British Museum).

At the junction of Rectory Road and the High Street, standing on the corner is Bluntisham House, once the rectory. It stands well back with lawns, flower beds and thickets sloping down to the road. The house has a Georgian front with a rather ornate stone doorway taken from the Old Slepe Hall in St Ives. It looks a suitable setting for one of the detective stories written by one of its former occupants – Dorothy L. Sayers, whose father was rector here from 1897–1918.

In the High Street is the picturesque Rectory Cottage, with timber framed gable end and typical Huntingdonshire mansard roof. Beyond this is the old village school, now used by the play group. Opposite is the non-conformist Meeting House and its Sunday school, where Belgian refugees were housed in the First World War. Just to the right of the chapel is Meeting Walk, now a pleasant footpath through the centre of the village. It is said to have originated from the special path used to take coffins to the churchyard for burial avoiding, as far as possible, inhabited or frequented parts of the parish on which the passing corpse might bring bad luck.

The home of the Tebbutt family for about 150 years is called Walnut Trees after the two trees which stand opposite. Outside on the wall of the house is an elaborate sign which was made by Pittoors, an ornamental ironworker, who with his wife and four sons were refugees from Belgium during the First World War. He was provided with a small forge and a supply of Swedish iron. This craftsman produced beautiful work, the sale of which helped to keep him and his family.

Mill Lane was the site of the mill from 1608–1899. It had a dark tradition connected to the old mill of long ago and a ghost was said to be seen. The last miller would not stay in the mill at night on his own. Now on certain nights it is said the sound of the wind in the sails can still be heard.

St Mary's church was first started in 1330, with the chancel and north chapel or vestry. Various monies had been left for the teaching of the poor of the whole parish. A room under the tower of the parish church was used as a schoolroom. The church is said to sit on the boundary of Bluntisham and Earith.

A curious local custom existed whereby a bride could free herself of all debts incurred before her marriage, by walking across the road naked to her husband's house!

Bottisham ᘛᘚ

Bottisham is very much a 'fen-edge' village, built along the line of a small ridge, slightly higher than the surrounding fens, thus making the village long and fairly narrow. The parish church is only 51 feet above sea level. In more recent times, land on which some of the village is built was owned by St Bartholomew's Hospital and two cast iron posts in the garden of Parsonage Farm record this fact.

The village contains some notable old houses, Stocks – once a village shop and now a restaurant, Tudor House, Bottisham Place, the old Court House and an unusual group of cottages called The Arch. The Grange which now serves as a private residential home for the elderly was the vicarage and Bleak House was used for a time as a private school. The 13th century church of Holy Trinity is said by Pevsner to be 'one of the most interesting churches in Cambridgeshire.'

Judging by reminiscences, even in the hard times of the 1920s and 1930s, life was never dull. Harry Morgan and Alfred Arber, schoolmaster and parish clerk respectively, dispensed discipline in their spheres and earned the affection of generations and have passed into village folk-lore. Perhaps the geographical location, midway between Cambridge and Newmarket with their two contrasting cultures gave the village its vitality.

The vast change, within a lifetime, from a rural community of about 700 to the present 2,000 or more seems to have been caused by a series of friendly 'invasions'. Each one has added to the enormous range of occupations, interests and talents which is now enjoyed.

The first was educational, when in 1937 the second Village College in the county was built. It was one of the Countrymen's Colleges as envisaged by Henry Morris. When it opened it served as a centre for 11 villages with a population totalling 7,000 as a school in the daytime and as a 'University' and social centre in the evenings when parents attended.

The wartime invaders were the Tank Corps, the RAF, evacuees and finally 1800 Americans. Some of each group formed lasting ties with the village people.

The post-war building boom brought new faces with each small development until the large Park Estate brought a flood of newcomers – almost literally, as they stepped straight into a world of mud and wellies, because of a reluctance to make up the roads. As the number of residents grew more shops opened, better medical services were necessary and a new Family Practitioner Group Practice, including a baby clinic was built, a playgroup and nursery school opened, a separate primary school was built and gradually the old and the new have merged to make a village well provided for and acting as a centre for the surrounding smaller villages.

The village can claim a distinguished 'first'. MAGPAS – the local flying doctor service – was the brainchild of Dr Silverston MBE who practised here for many years but now, in his retirement from General Practice concentrates on the organisation of the life-saving service.

Boxworth 🍂

A 'small well wooded village' has been an apt description of Boxworth since the earliest records of 1086, when it was spelt Bochesworde.

The one important building is St Peter's church, of early Norman origin, which once had a spire, destroyed in a gale and replaced by a castellated tower, Two famous scholars are associated with it; John Bois (Boyce) was rector here from 1595 to 1637 and translated the Apocrypha for the King James version of the Bible. He died in 1643 aged 83 and was buried at Ely.

By the altar is the burial stone of Nicholas Saunderson, FRS blind from birth, but who became Professor of Mathematics at Cambridge University. His horse took him into Cambridge and back to Boxworth each day. The incumbent of St Peter's since 1961 is the Reverend Hugh Mosedale.

The outline of the old medieval village can be seen in fields near the church, as hollow ways, 'ridge and furrow' ploughing, crop marks etc. Overhall Wood with the remains of its old manor and moat is well known for its oxslips and bluebells, its bird life and badger colonies. In the woods in Boxworth live wild deer, such as muntjac and roedeer.

The Boxworth Experimental Husbandry Farm of great renown is to be found in Battlegate Road. This gives employment to some of the villagers, others being employed on local farms. A small number commute to Cambridge.

The oldest family in Boxworth is that of the Thornhills. They bought large estates in 1785 and Edmund Henry Thornhill came to live in the manor house in 1884. The present inhabitant is Edmund Basil Thornhill, who, when he celebrated his 90th birthday, entertained at the manor many of the 'old' village people. The present lord of the manor and patron of the church living is his son, George Edmund Peter Thornhill of Newark.

Old documents relating to Boxworth from the 13th century onward have been transcribed and collected in book form to be seen in the County Records Office, the University Library and the Society of Antiquaries in London. Village 'bygones' have been assembled at Church Farm. These include the old bakery dough trough, old farm implements, as well as Victorian domestic items and clothing.

26

Brampton

Situated now within the triangle formed by the A1 (Great North Road), the A604 (Huntingdon/Thrapston road) and the A141 (Huntingdon/Buckden road), Brampton was mentioned in the Domesday Book. The name is a corruption of Brantune, a place of bramble bushes. Its population has grown from 780 to 1801 to 4510 in 1981.

The manor of Brampton was one of the Royal residences. Brampton Wood, to the west of the village, is one of the few remaining areas of the Forest of Wabridge which at one time stretched from Stamford, Lincolnshire in the north down to Oxfordshire. There was excellent hunting. The Manor ceased to be a private residence in the early 1960s and will become the Cheshire Home for Cambridgeshire and Bedfordshire.

The parish church stands guard at the east end of Brampton, a fine building parts of which date from the early 14th century. Local 'notables' are buried here – the Earls of Sandwich, Brigadier General Robert Bernard Sparrow, and his wife Lady Olivia Bernard Sparrow, a great benefactress to the village. She founded the school, the Round House, built as an infirmary, octagonal in shape because for reasons of economy there was one central fire to heat the six two-bedded rooms. She purchased a property to be used for the education of girls in the parish and also built a number of cottages for farm labourers and their families.

There are a few listed buildings but the only one with a claim to fame is Pepys House. It was at one time owned by a relative of Samuel Pepys' family, but the diarist himself lived there for a time and often visited in later years.

One of his favourite haunts was the Black Bull, a coaching inn and the oldest in Brampton. Of the 12 known to have existed, only four remain, of the rest five have ceased trading within living memory although happily two have survived as private residences.

The main occupation in the area had been farming although in the 1920s and 1930s there was a large nursery which supplied rose bushes world-wide and in one particular year a quarter of a million bushes were sent to local authorities in Canada. The rambler, *Dorothy Perkins*, was bred here.

There has been an RAF presence in Brampton since 1940 although the station was not permanently established until 1957 and this is now a major employer. Its establishment as well as the improved road and rail links with London have played a part in the residential development of Brampton.

Buckden ✒

Buckden was the principal residence of the Bishop of Lincoln for seven and a half centuries, mainly because it was in the centre of the diocese. Considerable portions of the episcopal palace remain. The Great Tower stands with its four turrets as does the Gate-house, connected with the Tower by a curtain wall, and the outer arched gateway with a high battlemented wall surrounding the south west corner of the grounds. The Towers, as it is now known, is owned by the Claretian Missionaries who have built a chapel adjoining the Great Tower. Outlying portions of the episcopal demesne include the Vineyards, now the village playing fields, and Lion's Wear, a narrow strip of meadowland through which a pathway runs from Lucks Lane to the Vineyards.

Adjoining the palace is the parish church of St Mary. The chancel and porch are 13th century and the nave 15th century. During the time of Cromwell the rood and most of the stained glass was removed. The main door still hangs on its original hinges. Opposite the church is the Old Vicarage – a new vicarage was built in recent years on land owned by the Towers – and the manor house, now divided into several residences.

There are several fine residences, among them the Red House and Ivy House in Church Street, the White House in Mill Road, Jessamine House and the Coneygarths in the High Street, and Field House in Silver Street. Public houses used to abound but these are now reduced. Six have gone. Those remaining are the Spread Eagle, the Falcon, the Vine and the two great hostelries, the Lion and the George. The Lion was once a guest house attached to the Towers. Next to the George is the old forge with the village fire rakes on the wall.

Schools were run in the village in previous times but the present school dates from 1871. It has been greatly enlarged since the 1950s and now has 350 primary pupils. It stands adjacent to the village green, originally a pond but filled in by a local farmer prior to Edward VII's coronation for which the present trees were planted.

There has been much building during the last quarter of a century. There are two sets of almshouses in Church Street run by various charities.

People living in Buckden are catered for by three grocer's shops, a butchery, a bakery, two newsagents, a health food shop, a hairdresser, a dress shop, a jeweller and other services. There are two builders. Farming has always been the foremost livelihood and there are eight farms. Gravel workings have denuded the parish of considerable agricultural land in the north-east adjoining the river Ouse.

Burwell ❧

Burwell is a large village near the Old Fen, located some twelve miles east of Cambridge and four miles north of Newmarket. The population is around 5000 and is expected to grow, as more houses are being built according to a set village plan.

Burwell is two miles long and has two distinct areas, High Street and North Street and Newnham which are linked together by the Causeway. North Street and Newnham are former commercial areas associated with water transport on the Lodes. Hythe Lane would have led to the The Hythe which was a loading place for barges.

St Mary's church, a fine 15th century building in the Perpendicular style, stands in the High Street. There is evidence of Norman work in the tower. Extensive restoration has been carried out on this building over the past few years. In the churchyard can be seen The Flaming Heart tombstone marking the burial place of 78 persons who died in a barn fire whilst watching a puppet show on 8th September 1727. It was never fully established whether the fire started by accident or was started deliberately by someone who had a grudge against the puppet master. Unfortunately the fire spread rapidly and the doors had been locked to keep out unwanted persons so the loss of life was great.

The site of Burwell castle adjoins the western side of the churchyard. The castle, started in the 12th century, was famous in the reign of King Stephen, because during a siege the notorious Geoffrey de Mandeville was slain. Only the moat now remains with the spring which filled it, hence the site is known as Spring

Close. The Mandeville name lives on in a road behind the church.

There are many old and interesting buildings in the village including the manor house and Maltings Corner in the High Street, a long stone building, The Old Priory once known as the Parsonage, and the Tunbridge in Low Road.

As well as its agricultural background, Burwell has always been a place of industry, digging of turf (peat), cement making, quarrying clunch for house building and making of chemical fertilizers were all carried on in the past. Now agricultural engineers and a factory making corrugated cardboard are among the chief employers, but many of the local people travel to Newmarket or Cambridge to work. At one time the Burwell and District Omnibus Company was run by a local family, but like the railway station which is now extinct Burwell and District Buses are no longer with us.

A Windmill Trust was set up and has restored an old windmill to working order, and the Museum Trust is converting a barn into a museum for the village.

Bury 🌿

Bury is situated on the very edge of the fens adjacent to Ramsey. It is an idyllic setting with the lovely church of the Holy Cross, parts of which date from the 12th century, standing on a hill overlooking the babbling brook and the golf course (it is called Ramsey Golf Course but most of the course is situated in Bury parish). Bury church has one piece of furniture so special that it has been borrowed by the Royal Academy of Arts for an exhibition. This is a lectern, not in the shape of an eagle like so many, but more box-like with a single leg and a stone base, and intricately carved.

The old stone-built two-room school in the High Street is now converted to a dwelling house and the school removed to a new building in Owls End. Bury has expanded rapidly since the 1960s and is still growing. There were 496 voters on the electoral roll in 1967 and 1094 voters in 1987.

Most of the residents' everyday needs can be met in the village by the long serving local businessmen. The dairy has been in the same family for nearly 60 years. Nowadays it is only a retail business as they no longer keep and milk their own cows. The buttercup fields where the cows used to graze are full of houses. The sub-postmaster has been selling stamps etc for over 30 years while the owners of the other village shop have been here over 20 years. The owners of the garage on the corner have also been here over 20 years and the publican at the White Lion has over a decade of service to the village!

Castle Camps ✺

Tucked away in the very south-eastern corner of Cambridgeshire, Castle Camps borders onto both Suffolk and Essex with tranquil rural landscapes from the village over all three counties.

The village name derives from ancient earthworks and a subsequent Norman castle whose moat can still be discerned from the air. A Norman church – All Saints – remains at the castle site which is one of the highest points in Cambridgeshire (a giddy 415 feet above sea level!). The present village is about one and a half miles from the original site; the residents decamped in the 17th century to avoid the worst ravages of the plague, and gave rise to Camps Green (which still appears on some maps).

Castle Camps has always been a farming community, but unlike today with its sizeable commuting population, most villagers used to work on the surrounding farms. Indeed, there are village residents who can still recall long hours of hard manual labour using horses and the subsequent steam machinery right up to the highly mechanised farming of recent decades. Originally the land was given to the De Vere family by William the Conqueror. It remained with this family (the Earls of Oxford) until the reign of Elizabeth I when it passed to the Skinner family, a London merchant son of a Lord Mayor, and thence to the Charterhouse Trust from whom current farming families, such as the Haylock family, purchased it.

Although only some four miles from Haverhill, Castle Camps is fairly isolated, only gaining the telephone in the early 1930s, piped water in 1937, and electricity in 1949. The relative isolation has probably contributed to the close community structure.

There are some local legends. An unidentified soul is said to be interred in Wigmore pond, now filled in and a ghost is reputed to haunt 'Owl's Hoot' cottage where a husband and his sister allegedly murdered his wife.

In comparatively recent times, workmen carrying out alterations at nearby Shudy Camps Park uncovered a priest's hole which had hitherto remained undiscovered. There are also sporadic references to a tunnel from Camps Castle to Hedingham Castle but evidence is hard to establish!

With regard to famous people associated with the village, the rector John Body wrote the hymn *O Jesus I Have Promised* in the 1860s, otherwise the villagers are content to savour the delights of village life, generally keeping the good life to themselves in their relatively unspoilt environment.

Castor & Ailsworth 🎋

Four miles west of Peterborough are the two villages of Castor and Ailsworth. There is no visible boundary between them except the village sign set up by the WI to commemorate their Golden Jubilee. Each village has its own character and identity although they always shared the church and school. Ailsworth was originally a Saxon settlement and Castor named after 'Castra', a Roman camp. Ermine Street, the Roman road, crosses the Nene Valley in a north westerly direction through the cornfields. The area around the road was the site of potteries where the distinctive Castor Ware was made. Many of the pots and jugs are decorated with hunting scenes in colour-coated ware. This must have been a very prosperous place as a magnificent praetorium was built across the top of the hill where the church now stands. Excavations have unearthed baths, fine wallplaster, mosaics and many burials.

Ailsworth (the spelling of which has varied over the years), was a farming hamlet when in Saxon times Kyneburgha and her sister founded a nunnery in the ruins of the Roman house. Many artefacts including a comb, brooches, pins and domestic ware were unearthed among traces of humble wooden huts. The sisters' father was Penda, king of Mercia.

The 12th century church was dedicated to St Kyneburgha and is a fine example of Norman building. The magnificent tower has tiers of double arches with carved heads; the spire is a 14th century addition. Over the chancel door can be seen a Latin inscription which reads 'This church was dedicated on April 17th 1124'. Inside, on the north wall, can be seen a panel of three wall paintings depicting the martyrdom of St Catherine at the wheel, reputed to be one of only two known to exist.

Much of the 'old' villages still remains, stone built houses and cottages, thatched or roofed with Collyweston slates. Some have been 'improved' beyond recognition, some demolished to make room for more modern developments, barns converted and most of the old stack yards infilled. Two paddocks, one in each village have been preserved and are watched over with great care; these allow us the opportunity to see animals and keep our rural connections. There are still four village inns, two stone built and thatched maintaining their olde world charm, the others of mixed style but all offering their own special characteristics. Village Farm House, mostly 16th century, still has an Anglo-Saxon window and a dovecote mentioned in the Domesday Book; Castor House is Georgian; The Cedars, once the home of William Le Queux, (author of *Rasputin*) is 18th century; and the village hall was once the National School built by Lord Fitzwilliam in 1829.

Ailsworth village green sports a most magnificent horse chestnut tree planted on the site of the old village pond. It is a sheer delight when seen in full bloom, dressed overall in pink and white candles. Just round the corner is the Methodist chapel, an oasis of village life, where Sunday services have been held since 1860; the school-room at the back serves many purposes but on Sundays reverts to its rightful role.

Catworth 🐟

Catworth, or Cateworth as it was known in the 13th century, also includes the hamlet of Little Catworth. The village lies in the middle of the parish on the road from Kimbolton to Thrapston – part of the old coach road from London via St Neots to Oundle.

The church is in the middle of the village and near to it are Glebe House (the old rectory), the former school which is now the village hall, and several 17th and 18th century houses.

At Brook End, about a quarter of a mile west of the village, is Brook House, added to and enlarged by Sir Felix Booth (about 1850), distiller and alderman of London. It incorporates part of a 16th century house and the hall has the original fireplace.

Long ago a bell was rung every day at noon, maintaining a tradition that a stranger found men making hay on a Sunday, not knowing what day it was. He therefore left money to have a bell rung at noon on Saturday, that they might recognize the day.

Now Catworth is in the commuter belt, and the village has expanded in some ways and shrunk in others. In the not very distant past, there were three public houses, an off licence, three bakeries, two stores and a butcher's shop. Now we are down to one village store/post office, one public house (the Racehorse) within the village plus the Fox, a mile away on the A604 but still within the parish, and a petrol station/garage workshop. Many old houses remain and gradually modern houses and bungalows have crept in.

The church is 13th century and is beautiful inside and out, with fixed pews and an impressive brass chandelier holding candles.

The lovely village sign on the small green greets folk as they enter from the busy Kettering Road. It depicts the important farming industry of a village surrounded by three large farms.

Chesterton 🌿

Chesterton has been occupied since pre-historic times. The Roman farm site at Arbury gave the village its name. For many centuries it was an agricultural village but had strong connections with the barge traffic on the river Cam, the barges coming from as far as Kings Lynn, and with the famous Stourbridge Fair for which it was the most important crossing of the river. Until quite recently, well in living memory ferries took folk across the river from Chesterton to the Stourbridge Common side, making it quicker to reach the town of Cambridge. Its many inns, some now gone, must have provided accommodation for many visitors who came to the fair not only from this country but from many parts of the world. The fair was very well known.

The river is the most prominent feature in Chesterton where the earliest settlers first built their homes. It is now a very large spread out village, indeed it is hard to decide where Cambridge City ends and Chesterton begins!

Chesterton possesses many fine houses of differing architectural periods, one of which is reputed to be the oldest house in the area, at least by Chesterton inhabitants! It is well worth a visit even just to look at from the outside, and is placed not far from the parish church of St Andrew. It is called Chesterton Tower. Previous owners included the Abbot of Vercelli, in Northern Italy, whose representative lived there in 1279 approximately.

Chesterton Hall is another fine old house dating from about 1650. It was much larger years ago and stood in extensive grounds. It is a fine Jacobean building built of red bricks. A Mayor of Cambridge once lived in this house but now what is left has been changed into flats by the City Council.

The parish church of St Andrew, with its fine spire has been the centre of worship for more than 700 years. Inside a very interesting Doom painting stretching over the chancel arch can be seen. Outside to the left of the porch is an unusual wall tablet commemorating the death of a young child who was the daughter of a freed African slave married to an Ely woman. There are also many interesting gravestones from which local history can be gathered including one to Benjamin Jolley, known as Charon, a ferryman at the Pike and Eel (which is a public house) for over 50 years. Many tales can be told about the ferrymen. Sadly one ferry sunk and lives were lost.

Other religions are catered for in the village. It once had several chapels one of which is now the Chesterton Workingmen's Club. It has a new chapel in Green End Road, where once a huge Iron Age hoard was found.

At the 'newer' end of Chesterton off Milton Road St George's church can be found. This was built in the 1930s to serve the ever growing population at this end of Chesterton.

Chesterton has fine nursery, infants and primary schools, the latter being St Andrew's Community School which was recently built to replace the old Victorian school which stood in the High Street opposite the shops, where now the houses in Primary Court stand.

Cheveley ✤

Cheveley lies to the south east of Newmarket, off the B1063 road. Over one hundred years ago an anonymous poet left a record of his native village. He described the ruined castle in the park, near to which the Duke of Rutland's mansion stood, 'who visits it every year'. The long street of the village, with its neat, small cottages, its village school, post office, shops, chapel and pub called The Star is captured in verse. There was a blacksmith's shop too, 'and the name is Johnnie Deer'.

These verses, written by an unknown person in the late 1870s, could easily be used as a guide for a stroll through Cheveley village today. Naturally change has come – gone are the mansion, the forge and the little shops while new houses have been built and tiles have replaced some thatched roofs. Agricultural land is now used by the many stud farms in the area for rearing racehorses. But the 12th century flint church with its unusual octagonal tower and attached barbican still stands proudly in the middle of the village and trees and green fields abound. It is to be hoped that as the village is not on a main thoroughfare it will long maintain its attractive air of calm and tranquillity.

Christchurch

Christchurch is a small village situated in the heart of the fens, in what used to be known as the Isle of Ely. The surrounding fens have some of the richest and most productive soil in the country, so farming is naturally its main industry, growing mainly corn, sugar beet and potatoes. Before the Second World War, almost everyone living in the village worked on the land, but since the introduction of modern machinery, very few workers are employed on the farms now.

In the early days the village was known as Brimstone Hill and belonged to the parish of Upwell, until the parish of Christchurch was created with the building of the church in 1865. For a long time Brimstone Hill remained, but the origin of the name is still a mystery. Some say it is from the Brimstone Butterfly which inhabited the hill.

The Townley family financed the building of the church, as well as the village hall, formerly known as The Men's Institute. The village school built in 1932 is known as the Townley School, and the family coat of arms is on the school and the village sign, which was provided by the WI. The workmen's hut used while building the church was sold when the church was completed and purchased by the village carpenter Mr John Hiam, who moved it across the road and used it for his home. He named it The Ark, and it is still standing today.

Rev. Sayers was rector of Christchurch between 1917 and 1928. His daughter Dorothy L. Sayers was the author of many novels, in one of which, *The Nine Tailors*, Christchurch was mentioned.

There was a village blacksmith, Mr J. Rolfe, who was kept busy shoeing horses and repairing farm equipment. After the Second World War, his two sons Wolsey and Jack joined him, but the blacksmith's work began to change as tractors and modern machinery began to take over on the land. The workshop still remains in the village but is no longer used as a blacksmith's shop.

Water was piped to the village in 1912 and to locals it was known as Marham water because it came from a spring in a small Norfolk village called Marham. This too, was another gift from the Townley family. Many years later, in 1949, electricity was brought into the village. Today, there is a post office, a well stocked shop and many activities for members of the community to take part in.

Coates 🦚

The very pretty village of Coates is on the A605 between March and Peterborough, on the northern edge of the fens, and is about ten feet above the surrounding areas which are five feet below sea level.

As late as the 1940s the main occupations were agriculture and the brickworks at Kings Dyke. There were four shops, four public houses, a blacksmith, miller, thatcher, cobbler and two carpenters that were also undertakers. Today there are three shops, two are general stores, one of which houses the post office and the third is a butcher's. Two of the pubs have been closed and the other businesses have gone. Taking their place are two garages and a farm machinery sales and repair organisation.

Coates has one of the largest village greens in Cambridgeshire. The main road divides it in half. North Green is surrounded by very old large lime trees, but both greens have a variety of younger trees. In the past donkeys, horses and geese had the right to graze the greens. This finished when modern day traffic made it dangerous.

Old houses surround the greens, but most of the old thatched cottages have gone and new have been built in the spaces. Fortunately the new housing estates are behind the older properties.

The church is on the west side of North Green, with the church hall, the graveyard and the old rectory. The church was built in 1840. In 1987 a new rectory was built.

The chapel is a severe square building in the centre of North Green and was built in 1840 just before the church. Some villagers objected to the building, and during one night pulled down the work of the previous day, so chapel folk guarded the building until it was completed. It was enlarged in 1866.

The public house named The Carpenters Arms but known as the 'Top House' by locals is by the main road. Seats, swings and slides are on both greens. A very pretty lane called Cow Way leads from the bottom of North Green to the back of the village of Eastrea, about one mile away.

The Vine public house is on the South Green and close by is the old fire engine house, about the size of a modern garage. The engine was pumped by hand and also pulled by the men, later by a pony called John Willy.

A very impressive village sign with scenes of long ago, horses, donkeys and geese on the green with the church on one side and the chapel on the other, is one of the best to be seen in the area.

Approximately three quarters of a mile from the village is a small lane to Eldernell, where many centuries ago there was a Roman settlement. Now four farms and a ruined house that is said to be haunted, because a man and woman killed themselves in a bedroom, make up this pretty area that leads to washland. This often floods. Once it was all grassland but some of the land is now arable and very fertile too.

Colne 🍃

Colne is a very ancient settlement and probably got its name from the Latin word 'colonia' which means a colony. Two fairly large Romano – British sites have been excavated within the parish.

It has always been an agricultural village but with the coming of the railway, fruit became an important crop. This is no longer so as more farmers are turning their orchards over to cereals, sugar beet and other crops.

For some unknown reason the centre of the village has moved. The original church site, the moated site of one of the manor houses and the workhouse are a quarter of a mile from the present village centre. The time and reason for this move is unknown. The tower of the original church fell down in 1896 and demolished most of the building. Permission was given for a new church to be built in the centre of the village. The £600 needed to build this new church was raised and the building consecrated in 1900. Stones from the old church were incorporated in the new one. It is dedicated to St Helen. The small green in front of the church was originally the village pond and was filled in during the late 1960s.

Colne inhabitants were very prominent in the rise of Nonconformism in the area. They were particularly involved in the Baptist chapel at Bluntisham and eventually built their own small Baptist chapel in 1869. It is now a private bungalow.

The village was well served with public houses – there were eight in 1881 in a village of less than 400 inhabitants. Some had unusual names, such as The Spade and Bechet and The Red, White and Blue. The Green Man is the only one still a public house.

The village suffered from a serious fire in 1844, started by a disgruntled labourer from Bluntisham. Consequently, few very old houses remain.

A road in the village, close to the new church, is named after the family who owned one of the three Colne manors. Drury Lane is so named after the Drury family whose London house was situated in a road of the same name.

Comberton 🦢

Comberton is on the former main railway route from Cambridge to Oxford. The local pronunciation is Cumberton. The Domesday Book shows a population of around 200 in the 11th century.

William the Conqueror granted the manor of Comberton to Erchanger, the baker. In return, he or his descendants baked a simnel cake each day for the king until 1270 when the frequency was reduced to one per week.

In 1863 the *Cambridge Chronicle* reported a case of witchcraft in Comberton. On 28th February 1863 an inquest was held on Emma Rust, aged 18, who had died from a succession of fits. The witnesses believed that she had been bewitched by a Mrs Stonebridge but were unable to say by what means this had been achieved.

Before 1914 the village was self sufficient with a blacksmith, brewer, tailor, cobbler, farmers and farm labourers. Now few are employed in agriculture and there is little local employment except for small businesses, such as timber suppliers, glasshouse producers, plant nursery and commercial centre. The village has grown since the 1960s with new housing estates and the population now exceeds 3000.

The railway from Cambridge which passed near the village closed in 1967. The line is now the home for numerous 'dishes' used for research and observation in radio astronomy. This gives the area a look of fantasy.

The National School was built at the crossroads in 1846 and is now a nursery school. A turf maze, probably from the 17th century was in front of the main entrance. In 1908 it was recut in the playground but was later covered over when the school was extended in 1926. This village school was superseded by the Meridian School (so named because the Greenwich meridian passes nearby) in 1968 and the Village College was opened in 1960.

The village pond is at the centre of the village at the crossroads. The mallard and other birds make it an attractive feature. The small village green around the pond was formerly marked by a stone cross but now has a painted wooden sign. One side depicts Comberton Mill (blown down in the last century) and the other side, the distribution of the herrings from the Herringland Charity. This is the only local charity still in existence. The rent from eight acres purchased herrings to be given to the poor on Easter Day. Now the Parish Council distributes a token gift to needy villagers on Good Friday. The village sign was provided by funds raised for the Queen's Jubilee in 1977.

The parish church (St Mary's) celebrated its 700th anniversary with many varied events in 1987. It stands on high ground overlooking the village and surrounding countryside. Other interesting buildings are two dovecotes (converted to dwellings) and a number of picturesque thatched cottages.

Coton

'And Coton's full of nameless crimes', wrote the poet Rupert Brooke, but then he was prejudiced in favour of Grantchester, the better known village to which Coton was once joined.

It is situated some three miles west of Cambridge, a compact and convenient village of about 760 people with a fine new school, two popular pubs and flourishing village clubs and groups.

The name comes from the Anglo Saxon word cotes, as in

Domesday times it was only a collection of small cottages for workers on the several farms and has no hall or 'great house'. Those not employed on the farms worked in Cambridge and most still follow this pattern.

There are three large families; Sadlers, Cousins and Childerleys whose names have dominated all village lists and teams for many years. Indeed when one, Simon Childerley was landlord of the Plough Inn, he was able to field his own family cricket team made up of himself, the seven sons out of his eleven children and three grandsons! There is a story of another celebrated match on the recreation ground when the visiting scorer, after finding that the bowler and the wicket keeper were both named Cousins, asked the name of one of the fielders and learnt it was also Cousins. 'What relation are they all' he asked innocently and all the spectators roared 'cousins'.

Back in 1880 there was a series of unsuccessful lawsuits when, after extensive coprolite digging had taken place in the village, the owners of the disturbed land claimed compensation. After several tries they ended by appealing unsuccessfully to the House of Lords and used up most of the village's charity money to help meet their costs.

There used to be a village pond, fed by the many springs. In 1953 it was filled in to tidy up the green outside the churchyard and promptly resurfaced in the rectory cellars which then had to be filled up also!

Nearby there is an interesting medieval dovecote, now in very poor condition, which the Cambridge Preservation Society hopes someday to restore.

The church has a Saxon font and a Norman window and a memorial to Andrew Downs, one of the scholars to make the Authorised translation of the Bible in the early 17th century. He retired from Cambridge to Coton, died here and is buried in the churchyard.

Cottenham ✺

Cottenham is a thriving working village with a population of 5000 and many small businesses. It is a wedge-shaped parish of 7224 acres, two miles long, built above the 20 foot contour line and is on a long spur of lower greensand reaching out into the fens.

There is evidence of Roman settlements in the fens along the Car

Dyke where Romano-British pottery has been found. The name Cottenham is thought to have derived from the many early English settlers known as Cotarii and their dwellings called cotes. It was called Cotenham in the Domesday Book.

Cottenham has been historically connected to the Abbey of Crowland since Saxon times and it is thought that it is this tradition which connects Cottenham with the origins of Cambridge University. After the abbey fire in 1109 learned monks from Crowland came to reside on their estate in Cottenham and lectured in Cambridge to a large number of scholars.

In the early 14th century Crowland manorial records of Cottenham there first appeared mention of the Pepys family. They became bailiffs of the Cottenham estate for the Abbots of Crowland during this time until the end of the 16th century. One of their descendants, though not born here, was the famous diarist, Samuel Pepys. The present 8th Earl of Cottenham is directly descended from John Pepys of Cottenham who was the great grandfather of Samuel. The Pepys Charity, endowed by Katherine Pepys, the last member of the family to live in Cottenham, is still administered in the village to give financial help to young people for the purchase of books and tools necessary for their apprenticeships or further education on leaving school.

Calvin Coolidge, President of the USA (1923–29) was descended from the Coolidge family who originated in Cottenham. The church register records the baptism of John Coolidge in 1604. He crossed the Atlantic in 1630 to become one of the early New England settlers.

The present church of All Saints is built in the Perpendicular style of the 15th century with pineapple pinnacles on the tower giving it a very striking appearance when viewed from across the fens. The church building today requires much restoration work so the present congregation are heavily committed to fund raising efforts to help preserve it.

There are some very interesting 17th century houses left in the village and one that is thought to be late 16th century. Some of them have retained their thatched roofs.

Three disastrous fires in 1676, 1847 and 1855 destroyed much of the housing in the village on each occasion. These houses were rebuilt in the design of the time so that today many of the houses in the High Street are of a uniform Victorian design, built in the yellowish Cottenham brick made from the local clay dug from the clay pits in Ivatt Street.

Cottenham Racecourse is well known in East Anglia and holds point to point meetings each year. In 1870 the Prince and Princess of Wales (afterwards King Edward VII and Queen Alexandra) were present at the Grand National Hunt Steeplechases held on the racecourse.

The October Feast, an old custom, is still celebrated every year on the 1st Sunday after October 11th. A parade is organised and most of the local associations including the Cottenham WI enter a decorated float.

Farming has always been the main occupation of the inhabitants over the centuries from sheep rearing in Tudor times to dairy farming on the commons. A thyme-like herb grown on the commons flavoured the cows milk and this produced the famous Stilton-like Cottenham Cheese. Each house had its own cheese press and cheese making continued until the change over to arable farming after the 1842 enclosures and the Cattle Plague in 1865 which was the final blow to dairy farming in Cottenham. There is still a cheese press in one of the old houses in Cottenham.

Coveney & Wardy Hill

Coveney and Wardy Hill are two small villages set on 'islands' above the fen, a mile apart, about four miles west of Ely. The combined population is about 350. They are run as one parish, but are two completely separate villages in many ways. Coveney derives its name from 'island in the bay', and not from anything to do with witches, as many people would like to think. Wardy Hill comes from 'warden's hill' or look-out. Although Coveney has neither shop nor pub and the school closed in 1986, and Wardy Hill has only one small shop, run by Miss Houghton in the front room of her house, there is plenty going on.

The main industry in the villages is agriculture. There are many farms of various sizes and these are mainly arable – the crops grown are potatoes, sugar beet, corn and onions. Up until the 1950s most people in the villages worked on the farms, both men and women. The women usually did jobs like weeding, 'chopping out' sugar beet and helping with the potato harvest. As the farms have become more mechanised, not so many people work on the land.

Coveney is not mentioned in the Domesday Book, but was first mentioned in 1060 when the manor was given to Aethelswyth for life in return for her gift to Ely Priory of her life interest in Stetchworth. She settled in Coveney with her maidens to work at embroidery and weaving. Wardy Hill is first mentioned in a document in 1251 – but there must have been a settlement here long before, as Bronze Age shields and swords have been found in the area.

Coveney church of St Peter ad Vincula, dates back to the 13th century with building going on during the 14th and 15th centuries. It was thatched until 1896 when the tiled porch was added. Coveney and Wardy Hill have their own Methodist chapels and Coveney also had a Baptist chapel which was in use from 1833 to 1906. This is no longer used, but can still be seen at the end of Mansion Farm house, and gravestones are still in the front garden. Mansion Farm is the oldest house in the village. It is thought to have been built at the same time as the church, and some of the fireplaces are built of the same Barnack stone. The roof is thatched, with a plaster front and many fine beams. The front door is very old and is still barred not locked. It is the only thatched house left in the village.

Another interesting building is the village pound found next to the pond. The date on the pound is 1840, but it is thought to be earlier. It was used to impound cattle that had wandered away from the common grazing areas.

Next to the pound is the village lock-up; this was actually used for housing the village bier which carried the coffins to church. The village pond and grass area around was cleared by the Parish Council in 1960. Here stands the village sign, presented to the village by the WI in 1977 to commemorate the Queen's Silver Jubilee; it is made of wood and was carved by Mr Carter of Swaffham in Norfolk. It is very colourful and shows Aethelswyth doing her embroidery, and a man from Wardy Hill looking out for cattle raiders coming across the fen. Wardy Hill has recently cleared its own village green and made a most attractive feature for the village.

Croxton

In August 1887 800 men and women sat down to a roast beef and plum pudding dinner at Croxton Park by invitation of Mr Newton, the owner of the house and most of the surrounding land. Children had tea afterwards and participated in sports, and there was dancing and fireworks until 10 pm, when God Save the Queen was sung. If you visited Croxton today you might wonder where all these people came from. Some would have been from Eltisley as the villages are very close and the owners of Croxton Park owned land in Eltisley and employed workers from there too, but it is apparent that Croxton is a village which until recently had a declining population.

Croxton village today mainly comprises two parallel roads running off the A45, plus a few houses along this busy main road, four miles east of St Neots and 13 miles west of Cambridge. One road, with the Spread Eagle public house on the corner, leads to Abbotsley; it has the lands of Croxton Park on one side and 20 houses on the other. The last two houses lie at the bottom of a hill and every spring hundreds of frogs cross the road here to find water to lay their spawn and then cross back again, and then a few weeks later hundreds of young frogs cross the road – drivers please take note and take care!

The other village road is the older inhabited part and leads to the gates of the Park and also to the church of St James. The church was built in 1280 but there had been an earlier church on the same site. Croxton has certainly changed – the original village was on a road between the church and where the big house stands but none of this village now exists at all. The last of the original village houses were demolished by the owner of the Park in 1780 and the site converted into a lake, but the village had been moving to its present position for many years before that. The present Croxton Park was built in 1760 by Edward Leeds but the Leeds family had lived there in an earlier house on the same site since 1571. The Leeds family owned the house, farmlands and virtually the whole parish, until 1825. Since then the land has been sold and divided, and several old 'estate' houses have disappeared. Among those left are a pretty cottage to one side of the Park gate and a late medieval timber framed house on the other side, facing a small green.

Croxton shares a rector with Eltisley, Graveley, Yelling, Tose-land and Papworth St Agnes, but a service is held in Croxton church every Sunday, and there is usually a full house for the Christmas candlelit carol service.

Doddington

'There are immense marshes, now a black pool of water, now a foul running stream, and also many islands...' wrote an 8th century monk of the area. Doddington is situated on one of those islands. The original parish of Doddington covered 37,801 acres, the largest in Cambridgeshire. In the Middle Ages, Doddington was one of the most important places in the Isle of Ely, but very few memorials of the past still exist. The only important pieces of architecture are the village cross – 14th century with a modern head, the remains of an early 19th century tower windmill, a round house, the clock tower and the church.

The church of St Mary the Virgin has a long history with the chancel and part of the north aisle dating back to the 13th century. The tower contains eight bells with dates ranging from 1736 to 1936. They are often to be heard ringing out across the fens as campanologists visit from all over the country. A famous rector of Doddington was Christopher Tye, the organist at St George's Chapel, Windsor. In 1560 he wrote the music for the Christmas carol *While shepherds watched their flocks by night*.

The village school bears the name of Lionel Walden who in his will dated 1719, directed that his property should be sold and the interest on the proceeds be allowed to accumulate until it reached £500. This sum was then to be used to build a school at Doddington.

Right in the centre of the village stands the clock tower, built to commemorate Queen Victoria's Diamond Jubilee. Originally it stood in the middle of the road at the junction of Benwick Road and High Street. Because of the increase in traffic, it was taken down brick by brick and rebuilt at the side of the road. In 1897 the clock had four faces, now there are only three.

Another interesting feature of Doddington is the 'Round House'. It was built in the days of mud and wattle, but was partly demolished in 1949. A new section was built on the back. It is the original round house, complete with thatched roof, that is seen from the road. Although it has all the conveniences of a modern bungalow, it retains its old world charm and is unique to the district.

As in most villages, farming is the main industry. Cereals, potatoes and sugar beet do particularly well in the rich fen soil. Some years ago a small brickyard provided work but all that remains now is Brickmakers Arms Lane and the brickyard pit. The pit is said to have been as deep as the church is high.

The biggest source of employment now is the hospital, which was opened in 1838 as the North Witchford Union Workhouse. In 1941 it was officially upgraded as a hospital under the wartime Emergency Medical Scheme. The local people are very proud of their little hospital. Over the years they have raised thousands of pounds to improve the facilities there.

The two public houses, The Three Tuns and The George are now as always, the hub of village life. As long ago as 1924 they had both installed wireless sets for the entertainment of their customers. They are home to the bowls club, the football club and numerous darts and domino teams.

Downham-in-the-Isle &

The first record of this village was when the manor of Dounham was given to the monks of Ely in the year AD 970.

The manor grew in importance during the Middle Ages when the 'Hall' or 'Palace' became the favourite residence of the bishops of Ely. It was at the end of the 15th century that the palace was reconstructed by the great Bishop Alcock. He was a discriminating builder and as Master of the Rolls one of the most important judges in the country. A chapel in Ely Cathedral is dedicated to him.

Perhaps the two best known bishops who stayed at Downham were Lancelot Andrewes and Matthew Wren. Bishop Andrewes was a great authority on languages and was responsible for translating the Authorised Version of the Bible from Genesis to the Second Book of Kings. Bishop Matthew Wren was a staunch Royalist and High Churchman. He was an uncle to the famous Christopher.

The ending of the bishops' regime in Downham came with the

arrival of the Dutch engineer Vermuyden and the fen drainage which revealed the rich black soil as we know it today.

There were few houses in early times but a lot of cattle and bulls. These were tended by a few men on stilts and they could cover the ground very quickly on these.

Later as the village grew there were more cottages, and many public houses, where quite a lot of drunkenness went on. From the 1890s to the Second World War years an annual feast was held the first Sunday in June, and for the following three days. On Feast Sunday, as it was called, caravans would roll into the village pulled by cart-horses. This was a most exciting time for children. On Feast Sunday, most homes had new potatoes (home grown of course) perhaps peas too and always gooseberry pie. Dad was a poor gardener indeed if he could not supply these!

Every January, on Plough Sunday, a plough is carried into the parish church of St Leonard for a service of blessing and prayers for the sowing and reaping of the crops in the coming year, also for the animals and all who work on the land.

Downham is still an agricultural village. Once much fruit was grown here in orchards and every cottage garden, but the orchards have now gone. Strawberries and raspberries are however very plentiful.

Downham has a few tales of ghosts, the most famous a monk who is supposed to appear in a certain bedroom of the old rectory and in the church grounds. One rector of not so many years ago, claims a bed was taken down in bits during the night and bells rang, but no-one was seen!

Duxford ✑

Duxford Parish is roughly triangular, about 3 miles long and 1½ miles at its widest point. Its northeast corner at Whittlesford Bridge holds Duxford's Chapel, an Ancient Monument, about 12th century, also the Red Lion public house, once a hospital for the Knights Templar. At this point it is about 80 feet above sea level. It rises to about 300 ft on Pepperton Hill, from where you can overlook the M11 motorway and 'Ciba Geigy' factory.

The present village is made up of two separate parishes – Duxford St Peter and Duxford St John, which accounts for the two churches both 12th century and the network of footpaths which used to run through the centre. St John's Church fell into disuse about 1877 and is now in the care of the Redundant Churches Council. The bells from St John's were transferred to St Peter's.

The majority of labour was centred on the farming community until the millers gradually changed from corn to grinding bones for fertilizer. In about 1853 one mill changed again this time to coprolite, also for fertilizer and the Cambridge Fertilizer Company was formed. This was taken over by Fisons Brothers and later still by Mr Sairling Rooke, this was the only attempt at manufacture until Mr N. De Bruyne started 'Aero Research' in 1934 now 'Ciba Geigy' (plastics). In the First and Second World Wars Duxford was used as an airfield and the population got steadily larger (now about 1750). The airfield is now occupied by the Imperial War Museum.

Duxford has had a village school since the mid 18th century. (The Cambridge Chronicle carried an advertisement for a School Master in about 1770). Lessons were held in a Vestry of St John's Church, but in 1847 the 'National School' was built in St Johns Street for 30 pupils. Later a headmaster and a school mistress were employed as pupil numbers increased, the headmaster living rent free in the adjoining house with an annual salary of £50.00, the school mistress earning £25.00. In 1960 another new school was built to take pupils from Duxford, Hinxton, Ickleton, and Duxford Airfield.

There are about twenty listed buildings in Duxford, probably the oldest of these being the Manor House in Green Street (14th century), and College Farm House next to St John's Church (15th century), both of which show timber framing of the original building. Both have been extensively altered, but by far the most noteworthy renovation is Duxford Mill, mentioned in the Domesday Book, but later burnt down and rebuilt in about 15th century with later additions in 16th century. This must be classed as a success story, as it was quite dilapidated and overgrown when Mr R. Lea took it in hand and recreated magnificent lawns, mill pool and superb rose gardens. It has had some notable visitors in its past. It is said that the inspiration for Charles Kingsley's book *The Water Babies* was gained here on one of his many visits. It is now open regularly to the public.

Earith 🎋

This is a small quiet village of around 3000 inhabitants. It lies twelve miles north of Cambridge, with the once county town of Huntingdon some twelve miles to the west.

Earith in some respects is the gateway to the fens and from its western elevated boundary, which incidentally runs right through the middle of the 14th century St Mary's church shared by the villages of Earith and Bluntisham, can be seen fine views of the fens to the Isle of Ely. Just below the church lies Bury and Little Fens, a scene of many memorable skating races and the birthplace of 'Bandy' or ice hockey. Even today, weather permitting, the Fen Speed Skating Championships are still held on this area of the fen, a far cry from the modern indoor speed skating as seen at the Olympics but equally, if not more so, as exciting.

The village, which is nestled between the watery junction of the Great Ouse river and the man-made Bedford Levels was once a highly developed inland port, hence the translation of the word Earith which means 'muddy harbour', and merchandise, usually timber was brought inland from the Wash. It was this timber trade which led to the great East Anglian firm of Messrs Jewson and Sons starting their business over 100 years ago and that timberyard and shop is still in existence and thriving in the village to this day.

The village during the 18th and early 19th centuries was one of great prosperity and the Earith Fairs were famous for miles around. Many a passing pedlar, cattle dealer or bargee would stop in the village to refresh himself at one of the numerous inns or public houses, most of which have disappeared today.

The village, although small has a history and charm all of its own. This part of the country being the birth place of Oliver Cromwell it has retained a great deal of the history of that period. Evidence of this can be seen by proceeding through the main street of the village to the river bridge, where on the far side looking towards Ely can be seen a large earthworks called 'The Bulwark'. This structure was built as a defensive fort to house cannon and the like to defend the waterways from the Royalists. Although the village is no longer a centre of trade and business, the population has not declined, in fact it has increased.

The modern village of Earith has tried to retain that all-important balance of history and progress. It has a modern school,

50

catering for both infant and primary education, a post office and general store, a local baker, a butcher's shop, a freezer centre and a ladies hairdresser. Efforts have been made to ensure that those houses that have been built or renovated in the main street through the village retain an appearance that is in keeping with their predecessors.

Elm 🌿

This now peaceful village still centres round its fine church of All Saints, much as it did 600 years ago. The church records go back that far, when there was both a rector and a vicar looking after the living. The Bishop settled a dispute in 1395 when 'unseemly bloodshed' had been spilt in the chancel over tithes, and finally the rector received 'all the tithes of sheaves of Wheat, Barley, Oats, Rye, Beans, Peas, Straw and Flax' while the vicar got 'all the Wool, Lambs, Calves, Porkers, Milk, Cheese, Bee's Honey and Wax'.

There was great parochial unrest when proposals were made to lay a tram-line through the village in 1881, even a petition sent to Parliament. The tramway was laid from Wisbech to Upwell alongside the canal. Alas neither have survived, the tramway was a victim of Dr Beeching and the canal was filled in when the Anglian Water Authority rerouted the drainage in the fens. Many of the villagers remember the tramway and the canal, which was well used in the past, particularly on Saturday nights when revellers came home from Wisbech by barge, singing all the way!

The schools have also changed. A hundred years ago only boys went to Elm and Emneth Church School and paid 2d a week, and the girls went to a private school situated where the present post office is today by Elm Bridge.

Many of today's residents were born here, married and stayed to have their families. Nobody wants to leave Elm and many want to come! There are of course more houses now, a change from the last century when the scattered cottages all had their own small-holding or at least a large cottage garden. It is still an agricultural area with fruit, vegetables, flowers and grains being harvested throughout the year, but most of the newcomers go further afield to work.

Social life centres round the church, church house, four public houses and the three village shops. In the 1920s there were five

51

bakers in the village and the smell of new bread was wonderful!

There have been changes, but in some ways the pattern of life does not change at all and in the old names such as Rose Lane, Halfpenny Lane, Begdale and Gosmore you can hear the ripple of the stream that once flowed through the village.

Elsworth 🌿

Elsworth lies on the western plateau, south of the Cambridgeshire fens, and has a population of over 700. This area was heavily wooded in ancient times, and, as its name implies, was a clearing in the forest owned by Eli, an Anglo Saxon chief. He probably settled here in the 7th century, travelling up the rivers from the Wash. The village developed along a brook which, before the draining of the fens, was probably navigable down to the Ouse. Today, the stream has shrunk to little more than a muddy water-course. After heavy rain, however, it rises rapidly and overflows its banks, exciting the children but frustrating the motorists who cannot reach their homes through the flood. Elsworth gives its name to an outcrop of limestone rock which can be seen in the bed of the brook at the south end of the village. It is full of molluscs and ammonites, and also in this area the vertebrae of an ichthyo-saurus and the leg-bone of a dinosaur have been unearthed.

All down the years Elsworth has been an agricultural village. In medieval times the Abbot of Ramsey was lord of the manor; everyone worked on the land and the chief crops grown were wheat, barley, peas and oats. Farming still dominates the scene, but fewer than a dozen living in the parish are farm workers, and the crops are reduced to wheat and rape. There are old men and women, born and bred in the village with their parents and grandparents before them, who hark back to the days of harvest homes and working horses. They tell of potato picking and threshing, of pea pulling and hedge laying and of other back-breaking jobs.

The last of the wheelwrights, John Throssell, died in 1988 at the age of 99. His business developed into carpentry and building, but there is still an Elsworth thatcher whose craft flourishes because of the demands for re-roofing from people who live in the restored 17th and 18th century yeomen's houses (now styled country cottages). There is a garage, the modern equivalent of the smithy;

a food stores which developed out of the 19th century butchery and is still in the same family of Knibbs; a post office and hairdresser, all of which would have been found here a hundred years ago.

Community life in the village is centred round the church, the primary school and the sports field. The church is 14th century and is notable for being almost entirely of one period. It is built of local field stone and local limestone rubble, and today the upkeep of its fabric drains the energies and resources of the rector and his parishioners. The sports field, or Grass Close by its old name, is the park of the manor house. The Manor was built in 1660 by Samuel Desborough for his second wife Sarah. It is now divided into four dwellings. Samuel was the brother of Cromwell's general, John Desborough, who married Cromwell's sister.

Elsworth is a thriving rural community, proud of its quiet heritage symbolized in the village sign. This depicts an ammonite, a shield bearing the arms of the Abbot of Ramsey, the Domesday Book, the church tower, sprays of wheat and a cartwheel. It was erected as a tribute to the aforesaid John Throssell, MBE, the parish clerk for 54 years, a fine craftsman and a true countryman.

Eltisley

Eltisley is a small village five miles east of St Neots and twelve miles west of Cambridge, by-passed by the A45. It is mentioned in the Domesday Book as Hecteslei, which means an Anglo Saxon settlement in a wooded area. There is still part of this ancient wood existing but now in private hands. The population has varied from 27 in 1086 to a maximum of 504 in 1871 and now stands at around 350.

The centre of the village is a beautifully kept triangular green surrounded by attractive houses and having three horse chestnut trees set, one in each corner. These were planted in 1887 to commemorate Queen Victoria's Golden Jubilee and are known as Faith, Hope and Charity. The green was common land and each April the parish council let it by auction for pasture. As recently as 1947 cows were walked along to the side greens to graze and goats were tethered there. In summer now the main recreation on the green is cricket.

Leading eastwards away from the green along Caxton End is a

line of lime trees known as the Row of Honour. These were planted during the First World War to commemorate each man from Eltisley who died. In January 1919 three trees were placed to form the Cross of Sorrow and in March 1919 the Peace Tree (an evergreen) was planted at the head of the line 'with the help of four brave survivors'.

An avenue of pollarded limes leads to the church of St Pandionia and John the Baptist, built c1200 near the site of a monastery which was among the oldest in England. Pandionia was the daughter of a Scottish king who fled to a kinswoman (the prioress of Eltisley nunnery) to avoid marrying the man chosen for her by her father. Pandionia died there and was buried by a well, which also carried her name. The well, in the churchyard, was a centre for pilgrimage till 1570 when it was destroyed by the rector, Robert Palmer, to 'prevent its use for superstitious purposes'. Her body, however, had been moved into the church in 1344.

Another legend which has grown up around the church concerns the famine in July 1234, when starving peasants raided local farmers' fields for food. The farmers were incensed and marched to the church the following Sunday and all, except one, asked the rector to excommunicate the offenders. He had hardly started to pronounce the sentence when a great storm blew up, destroying crops, livestock and buildings and devastating the whole area – with the exception of the lands and possessions of the one farmer who had not objected. These happenings are shown on the village sign.

Next door to the church is a large house built in 1612 by James Disbrowe, whose son John married Oliver Cromwell's sister Jane in Eltisley church in 1636. On the opposite side of the green is the oldest house in the village, built late 15th century, early 16th, and called the Old Post Office. Nowadays the post office is a modern shop on the north corner of the green across the road from the Leeds Arms, the only remaining pub out of five formerly in the village. The Leeds Arms was built in 1814 and also acted as a place where inquests were held in the late 1800s. The Cambridgeshire Hunt meets outside on Boxing Day, when the village is packed with people and cars.

Elton 🪶

Elton is situated on the borders of Cambridgeshire and Northamptonshire. Five miles to the east is the edge of the fens and to the west extends the area which was Rockingham Forest in medieval times. The river Nene flows through the valley at the lower end of the village and marks the boundary between the two counties.

Elton is a large parish extending to nearly 4000 acres. Fifty years ago Elton was a village very different from today, with five working farms and cows walking in all the streets to the farms to be milked. Today Elton is a dormitory village for Peterborough with new housing estates and old cottages and barns being refurbished, but still retaining its beauty with the village greens and lovely old chestnut trees.

Elton has been inhabited since pre-historic days. Early farmers settled in the parish nearby 6000 years ago and from then on agriculture has been most important to the village. There are five Roman sites in Elton and a major Roman road linking two important Roman towns which can still be traced through the eastern part of the parish. It was not until the Saxon period that Elton got a name similar to that which it bears today. The Saxon settlers laid out the parish boundary, built the church and set up two manors, and many of their fields carried on right up to the time when the parish was enclosed in the 1790s. There are two Saxon gravestones at the north side of the church.

One of the most notable features of Elton is the Park area, lying between the church and Elton Hall, which remains largely unaltered since the medieval period. It was possibly first created for deer hunting by the lord of the manor and was then converted for extensive sheep rearing. Later it was landscaped for the Earls of Carysfort who lived at the hall. Elton Hall was one of the manors the Saxons built – it was never a castle, but was defended. The hall for the last 400 years has been the home of the Proby family.

People who visit the hall can stroll along Overend and call in at the church. The tower of the church was probably built by the same man who built the Sapcot Tower at Elton Hall round about 1500 AD. Apart from the notable tower, the monuments of the Proby family and the William Morris stained glass windows – the church is very pleasant with commanding views to the west over the Nene valley.

One can walk down Middle Street, admire the stone and thatch cottages and on to the other end of the village where Stocks Green and its set of stocks lies. On the other side of the Green a watermill can be seen, which was mentioned in the Domesday Book. Nearby is the Crown Inn, set back from the green sheltering under the shade of the chestnut tree.

Eynesbury ✍

Eynesbury is divided from St Neots by the Hen Brook on the north side whilst the river Ouse separates it from Eaton Socon on the west side. The parish also contains three hamlets, Weald, Caldecot and Eynesbury Hardwick.

There is evidence of Eynesbury's early occupation in the Stone and Bronze Ages and the Iron Age. In the Roman and Saxon periods evidence shows the expansion of the settlement in both the Hen Brook and river areas.

As time passed the village developed into a pleasant one and as agriculture became the main form of livelihood several large farmhouses and farmyards were built. The cottages occupied by the farm workers were mainly terraced, but there were also some attractive thatched and timber framed houses, a few of these being lived in today.

In the oldest part of Eynesbury stands the church of St Mary, the register of which dates back to 1539. A Methodist chapel was built in 1855 and a new chapel built near the site of the original one in 1928.

In St Mary's Street in the past, sufficient small shops supplied the needs of the Eynesbury inhabitants and, as in neighbouring St Neots, there were many public houses. Several of these licensed premises survive today, serving the public with both food and drink, but the old shops have become updated or pulled down, and more traders have now opened premises to serve in various ways the ever growing population.

There still remain the two public open spaces which have been there for centuries. Eynesbury Green, on which May Day was annually celebrated, now contains several red chestnut and lime trees which are a delight in the spring and early summer. Eynesbury Coneygear, so named because it was a rabbit warren in the past, is a large open space near the river Ouse. Eynesbury Feast Day, the

Sunday nearest to the 8th September, used to be celebrated here.

The only really notable people Eynesbury can boast of are James Toller, the Eynesbury Giant, and the St Neots Quads. James Toller was born in Rectory Lane in 1798 and his height at the age of 18 was 8' 1½". In 1815 he was exhibited in London and there presented to foreign Royalty. He died in 1818, being then 8' 6" tall. In more recent times Eynesbury was put on the map because of the birth in November 1935 of the St Neots Quads, as they were always referred to. The four babies were born to Mrs Doris Miles, of Ferrera Avenue, with only the local doctor and midwife in attendance.

In the early 1960s St Neots, with Eynesbury, became a London Overspill area. There are now various factories and places of employment here, far removed from the agricultural industry which many older residents remember. In addition to the council housing estates, large private estates have been built.

Fen Drayton ✺

The traveller on the A604, seeking a break from the traffic and perhaps attracted by the distant spire of Fen Drayton church rising above the flat countryside, would be pleasantly surprised to find a small and tranquil village so near to the busy highway. A mile's drive would take him past the 'growers' area with glinting glass-houses full of chrysanthemums or tomatoes according to season and acres of fertile land planted with salad crops. These market gardens, each with its house, originally formed the Land Settlement Association of the 1930s, a government scheme to provide new employment for miners and others from the depressed areas of North Wales and the North East. They are now worked by individual tenants and the produce traded privately or on a collective basis. Some of the land has been sold for building but Fen Drayton is a 'conservation village' in the county's plan and new houses must be designed to blend in with the existing buildings.

Fen Drayton was mentioned in the Domesday Book. In 1448 Henry VI granted the land to Lady Margaret Beaufort, founder of Christ's College, Cambridge. It seems likely that from that time Members of the College would have decided to build here, the size and height of the dwellings demonstrating that the owners were men of substance. What is now the Three Tuns public house had its origins in 1420 and is popularly believed to have been the one-time meeting place for local merchants.

Since before the Norman Conquest there has been a church on the site of St Mary's, situated on one of the higher points of the village at 23 feet above sea level. The present building dates from the 14th and 15th centuries.

What appears at first to be a pretty stream flowing through the High Street is actually part of the drainage system which for centuries has been vital to this Fenland region. Although present day technology has reduced the danger of serious flooding, sandbags are sometimes delivered to vulnerable houses when the water level looks threatening. Many people have stories to tell of children being ferried to school by boat (and hugely enjoying the experience), and shopping being collected by boat. The disastrous floods of 1947 are vivid in the memories of all who experienced them. One of the new roads is named after Cornelius Vermuyden who came to the area from Holland in 1629 at the Duke of Bedford's request to direct a project of land reclamation. Visitors comment on the apparent Dutch influence on the style of the houses and a stone inscribed 'Niet Zondern Arbyt' (nothing is achieved without work) is incorporated into one fairly recently built house.

The original house to bear this stone was the parsonage inhabited at the beginning of this century by the Reverend Shaw and his 13 step-grandchildren. He was also Justice of the Peace and held his court in the summerhouse in his garden, disposing of those found guilty of drunken disorderliness or other undesirable behaviour into the village lock-up. This small two celled building still exists and today looks rather pleasant being situated on a grassy area in the centre of the village. It is windowless but with grids over each door and is furnished with benches.

Fenstanton ✍

Fenstanton with its population of approximately 2600 stands on the A604, nine miles from Cambridge and five miles from Huntingdon. The nearest neighbouring town is St Ives, the water meadows of which join those of Fenstanton. The village is well supplied with shops, and in the early morning the smell of freshly baked bread wafts temptingly on the air. The main source of employment in the village is the Unigate Dairies. The farms, having become so mechanised, now only employ very few men.

The parish church dedicated to St Peter and St Paul, built of rubble dressed with stone, is recorded in The Domesday Book of 1086. During the 13th and 14th century the church was enlarged considerably and a most beautiful chancel was built. On one of the chancel buttresses is an old mass dial, and near to it within the churchyard is the base of a stone cross, the date of which is unknown. Was it perhaps the old preaching cross, used before the first stone church was built?

In the centre of the older part of the village, at the bottom of the High Street stands the Clock Tower, built in the second part of the 1600s. This building has been put to various uses. At one time market taxes were collected there, at another period it was used as the village lock-up. The stocks are still kept within its walls, though thankfully not used in this day and age.

Fenstanton like many other places has played a part in England's history. During Cromwell's time in 1644, many of his men were stationed in the village. For providing food and shelter for one man, and food and stabling for his horse for ten days, 11 shillings was paid.

In 1620 John Howland, a resident of Fenstanton set out from Plymouth with the Pilgrim Fathers on the *Mayflower*. They landed at Cape Cod, Massachusetts and established the first permanent colony in New England. John Howland's mother and father lie buried in Fenstanton churchyard. In 1981 the Pilgrim John Howland Society in America gave a bell to Fenstanton church, so now there are six bells to peal out joyfully over the countryside.

In 1768 Lancelot (Capability) Brown, the famous landscape gardener, bought the manor of Fenstanton from the Earl of Northampton. Although he did not reside permanently in his manor house, he took a great deal of interest in his domain and he and his wife are both buried here.

Fenstanton is a lively village and all ages are catered for, from Brownies and Cub Scouts to senior citizens. The Morris dancers tour the village on Plough Monday and Bank Holidays, a happy and energetic sight.

Fordham 🪶

Fordham is situated between Ely and Newmarket. The name Fordham derives from a ford over the river Snail, which rises about two miles away.

At the beginning of the present century the population was about 1400 and it is now over 2000. Employment was mostly in agriculture and horticulture, and after the First World War flower growing for the cut flower markets was introduced on a considerable scale giving extra employment especially to women workers. Fordham flowers became well known in all the large markets in the country, while two transport businesses and two building firms also gave considerable employment.

There was at one time a Gilbertine Priory on or near the site of the present Abbey, where about a dozen monks resided and are said to have lived by working the land at the Bigging.

Fordham can boast having had a poet known as 'the rural poet of Cambridgeshire' but locally known as 'poet Withers'. He was the son of a poor shoemaker, who never attended school but was taught to read and write by his mother. His poems became famous. Queen Victoria sent him a gift of £50 and he received letters of congratulation from Charles Dickens, Martin Tucker

The village sign, Fordham

and many leading statesmen. The money he earned for his poems enabled him to move into a dear little cottage near the river known as Poets Cottage and indeed a relative of the poet still lives there. Poet Withers died in 1892 and soon after his death a public subscription fund was established which raised £54. With the money collected a stone monument was erected on his grave and a stained glass window was put in the church.

The parish church of St Peter is a beautiful building and the interior is maintained with loving care. It is partly Norman and Early English and the original work still survives in the nave. At the base of the tower a stone let into the masonry records that in 1901 a new clock and a new set of bell chimes were installed by public subscription in honour of the long reign of Queen Victoria.

The fine large village Victoria Hall was built to celebrate Queen Victoria's Diamond Jubilee and is in regular use. A large recreation ground was given to the village by the Dunn Gardiner family.

Fordham has a modern and thriving printing works, a bakery with bread and cakes made and baked by the third generation of the Palmer family, and Fordham Coaches provide us all with a cheerful service.

In the latter half of the last century at general elections fighting often took place between Fordham and Isleham men who had to come to Fordham to vote in the village school. On one such occasion the Riot Act had to be read outside the old school. It has now been made into four separate houses and a new school has been built.

Foxton

If you travel seven miles south on the A10 road from Cambridge you will almost certainly be stopped by the level-crossing gates at Foxton. However, the village is not on the main road. The heart of Foxton, half a mile away, is out of sight of the road and the railway. Station Road and High Street, an irregular 'T', form the skeleton of the village with occasional lanes and paths giving onto fields and farms.

There has been a settlement in Foxton since the Iron Age. Local author Rowland Parker, traced 2000 years of Foxton's history in his best-selling book *The Common Stream*. Thanks to his archaeological research and study of a mass of documentation more is known about the village's history than about that of many other villages. Even the village's name has changed over the centuries from Foxetuna in the Domesday Book to Foxtun in 1218, then it became Voxtun in 1300, Foxston in the 15th century and now Foxton, 'the farm where foxes abound'. Clunch stone, an early building material from the local hard chalk is very much in evidence. It appears as cottage walls topped by thatch or clay tiles, in garden walls, barns and pig stys. The groups of old cottages are interspersed with farm buildings, converted pubs and newer bungalows and houses. There are also occasional terraces of turn-of-the-century houses; these bear such names as Caxton, Chaucer and Byron Cottage and owe their existence to the 'Press' which stands by the war memorial at the junction of the 'T'.

The University Tutorial Press, its original title, was at first situated in East Road, Cambridge, but as it grew a larger site was needed and so in 1908 the works moved to Foxton. Today it has expanded further and is now known as The Burlington Press.

Between the yellow-brick council houses at one end of the village and the 1965 Georgian-style houses at the other there is a variety of styles illustrating almost every type of domestic architecture of the last 300 years. The church, the school, the White Horse pub, the shop and the large recreation ground, together make up the centre of the village and cater for the needs of all the inhabitants.

There has been a church on the site for over a thousand years. Six churches, if one considers each rebuilding as a new church. Foxton has had its share of less than worthy vicars and achieved notoriety in the 14th century when villagers violated sanctuary by dragging a murderer from the altar steps.

Opposite the 'Press' stands the school built over a hundred years ago in 1883 and still a very important part of village life. Its first headmistress, Miss Corlett, would surely be delighted as well as surprised to see her one-roomed school has several more bright, airy classrooms, a small swimming pool and a recently completed adventure playground!

Friday Bridge 🌿

The name of Friday Bridge must be known in some distant corners of the world for each year many young people, from such places as Turkey, Italy and the African continent, are attracted to the Agricultural Camp on the outskirts of the village.

Perhaps on arrival they look for a bridge. As no bridge is visible they may ponder on the name. There was once a bridge but it lies as an archway beneath the road and gardens near the clock tower. The entrance to it has been sealed with concrete. A bridge suggests water. Not too much of this can be seen either!

Not so far from the village centre are the droves and the fens like Laddus Drove, Maltmas Drove, Needham, Crowmere and Waldersea Fens. These names speak of earlier times when the shepherds and herdsmen drove their sheep, cattle, goats and geese along the trackways to graze on the open fen. Nowadays little stock appears to be raised, for the drainage of the area has meant the end of serious flooding and vast expanses of flat, fertile land available for cultivation. Thus, as well as a great variety of fruit and vegetables, there are acres of wheat, barley and sugar beet surrounding the village. These open spaces make the more noticeable great flocks of birds both on land and in the air.

St Mark's church has had its lopsided look almost since its erection in 1860. The church foundations were laid on peat. As the peat dried out or was dug up from the land round about, the church began to drop. The biggest movement took place in the first 20 years of the church's existence and in the dry summer of 1921. However, the building now remains reasonably stable so folk need feel no undue alarm when visiting this friendly church!

Just over a year after the ending of the First World War the then Vicar of St Mark's, the Rev. Covey Crump, stood on a lorry to pull away a Union Jack and unveil the plaque bearing the names of 24 men from the village who were killed in the war. The plaque is to be seen on the clock tower, erected as a memorial by voluntary public subscription.

One outstanding landmark is the water tower. This is a brick construction with some decoration and arched windows. It is difficult to believe it houses a gigantic tank holding some 100,000 gallons of water as it seems more like the keep of an ancient castle. From here the citizens of March, Wisbech, Chatteris and district obtain their fresh water. Under the turf beside the tower one million gallons are stored!

Two more modern buildings, not so outstanding in height, are the primary school and the community centre. About 110 children attend the school and enjoy its outdoor swimming pool at the present time. The community centre was a dream come true for some public spirited villagers when it was opened in 1984.

Fulbourn ∂🖗

The village of Fulbourn lies about five miles from the city of Cambridge. The name is derived from the Anglo Saxon 'Fugel-burn' meaning 'a stream frequented by birds'. How appropriate that a nature reserve is to be found here!

In the early part of the 16th century the village relied almost completely on agriculture but now is more of a dormitory village for the city of Cambridge. In 1851 the Electoral Register contained only 311 persons who were eligible to vote but in 1988 the total number of persons was 3059.

The most prominent feature of the village as it is approached from the city is the mill built in 1908. It is one of three smock mills in the county and is recognised to be one of the finest examples of 'Dutch work' in England, with three sets of stones. In 1933 it was struck by lightning and again three years later the fan tail was blown off in a storm. It finally ceased working in 1936 and is now being restored by members of the Windmill Society.

Fulbourn Manor is one of the oldest and most picturesque houses in the village and parts of it are of the original Tudor period. The manor passed to Richard Greaves Townley upon the death of his mother and there have been members of the Townley family at the manor ever since. Charles Watson Townley was Lord Lieutenant of the county and Richard Greaves Townley was the Member of Parliament for Cambridge from 1827 to 1852. The family have also been great benefactors to the village.

For many years the village had two churches in the same churchyard standing about nine feet from one another. However, in 1766 the tower of All Saints collapsed and in 1775 an Act of Parliament was passed to unite the two churches at the remaining St Vigor's. The lychgate was erected in 1923 in memory of the men of the village who fell in the First World War.

In July 1850 47 acres were purchased for the new Pauper Lunatic Asylum and the first patients arrived from the Hoxton Asylum in 1855. In 1922 it was renamed the Fulbourn Hospital and today houses psychiatric patients while the handicapped have the Ida Darwin Hospital and the Windmill School.

Fulbourn is a village of charm with plenty of old and thatched houses and cottages in a rural setting. The inhabitants are well catered for with a post office, chemist, butcher, newsagent, grocer and greengrocer. Four public houses remain of the nine or so of years gone by.

The elderly have 'Home Close', a residential home built in 1969 while the younger ones have an infant and junior school up to the age of 11 years. Older students move on to the Village College at Bottisham.

The community centre originally built as an infant school provides good amenities for village functions as does the Townley Hall.

Gamlingay 🦢

Gamlingay, the name of the village, is rather an appealing one and often causes speculation as to its origin. It does not mean gambolling in the hay as some of us were told when young! It is actually derived from the Saxon language and was known as Gamlin's Hae, which meant Gamlin's Island. This was because in those days most of the surrounding area was wet and marshy.

The Avenell family held one of the three manors in Gamlingay in 1308, and they helped with money when the rebuilding of the church took place. They held the manor for many years until the male line died out, and an Avenell daughter married into the St George family. The manor was eventually acquired by Merton College, Oxford, who still own land today.

A more recent famous son of the parish was squadron leader A. H. Orlebar who captained the victorious Schneider Trophy teams in 1929 and 1931, in the latter year winning the trophy outright. In 1929 he set up a world Airspeed record of 355.80 mph.

John Bunyan used to come to preach here and is reputed to have founded the Baptist Chapel here.

Perhaps the most momentous event in the history of Gamlingay was the Great Fire in 1660 which destroyed 76 houses and lost

Gamlingay its market which had flourished for many years.

The most important building is the parish church of St Mary the Virgin. According to Nikolaus Pevsner, it is the most impressive church in the area. In 1653 Miles Gray, the third member of the famous family of bellfounders, came to Gamlingay and cast five bells which he hung in the church tower. Three of these bells are still there today. Near the church is a splendid timber framed house known as the Emplins. The Cock Inn is at least 400 years old.

A medieval rhyme mentions the village approvingly –

> Sutton for mutton
> Potton for beef
> Gamlingay for pretty girls
> Waresley for thieves.

The Giddings

Great Gidding is a very old village on the remote rural western boundary of the county. The village straddles the B660 Kimbolton to Ramsey road. The long narrow properties at the top of the village are still known as the strips from the medieval arrangement of land management. The school founded by the Fitzwilliam family of Milton, Peterborough provides education for about 60 pupils. The 13th century church of St Michael has an octagonal wooden plaque on its chancel wall with a latin palindrome inscribed as a word square.

> SATOR
> ARIPO
> TENIT
> OPERA
> ROTAS

(This is thought to be a mistake; if the I's were E's this would work.)

Little Gidding is a tiny hamlet a mile south east of Great Gidding. It is widely known as the home of the Ferrar community. In 1626 Nicholas and his family, some 30 people gave up their brilliant positions in the world to lead simple practical Christian lives there. They taught the village children, nursed the sick, wrote and bound books and three times a day walked in procession from their manor to the tiny church of St John, the Evangelist in strict observance of the offices of the Book of Common Prayer. Only in this way, the Ferrars thought could any real protest be made against the scandalous religious bickering and cruelties which pre-occupied the country at that time. The experiment at Little Gidding made particular appeal to King Charles I and he stayed with the Ferrars on three different occasions, the last time as a lonely hunted man. One of the fields nearby is known as King Charles Meadow where it is recorded he once rode to Coppingford Grange after taking refuge from Cromwell's soldiers shortly before his capture. Some of the books written and bound by the Ferrar community are now in the British Museum. Nicholas died in 1637 and the Parliamentarian troops burnt the house and church in 1647. There is not a sign of the great house or gardens as T. S. Eliot wrote in his poem *Little Gidding*:

> 'Dust in the air suspended,
> Marks the place where a story ended'

The church was rebuilt in 1714.

In July 1937, a pilgrimage was organised by the Church Union, the organisation of the Anglo Catholics, to celebrate the 300th anniversary of the death of Nicholas Ferrar. Pilgrimages became a regular feature for several years with the meadows filled with visitors, gathered to pay homage to a man who made his faith a living force.

In 1938 Alan Maycock, an academic of Cambridge, published books about Nicholas Ferrar and the community. In his biography of Nicholas Ferrar he asked the rhetorical questions, 'Will the torch ever be relighted in this holy place? Will it ever be restored to God's greater glory and become once again a spiritual power house from which the church and her children may draw strength and inspiration?'

When he visited Little Gidding in 1946 with his wife Enid and friends, he found it in a very rundown and wretched state and wondered about forming 'The Friends of Little Gidding'. This was done on July 31st 1946 with the Bishop of Ely as president and Canon Jones, vicar of Great Gidding as warden. During the first five years, the church was repaired and refurbished and member-ship grew to over 200.

In 1968 Alan Maycock died, his biography of Nicholas Ferrar

was read by Robert Van de Weyer and in 1977 Robert and Sarah moved to Little Gidding to try to put the vision of Alan Maycock into practice.

This is now a modern ecumenical community, developing in the remaining buildings of the tiny hamlet and known as 'The community of Christ, the Sower'. In 1986 a second branch started, five miles away at Leighton Bromswold based on Castle House where the Van de Weyer family now live with other young people who wish to share the life of the community for a while. Other members live in the village nearby. Robert Van de Weyer is vicar of Great and Little and Steeple Giddings, Hamerton, Winwick and Upton parishes.

Girton ✤

In medieval times Girton was a typical English village, a prosperous and settled community. In 1279 the Hundred Rolls Survey gives a population of over 200. Towards the end of the Middle Ages the feudal society underwent change and so too do the names of the lords of the manors. The Trumpington family, who had owned most of the land for 300 years, faded away and new names appeared, such as the Cotton family.

The 17th century saw the drainage of the fens. The Cotton family showed great interest in agricultural experiments and consequently in the drainage of land around Girton. Although there were some substantial yeoman tenant farmers, Girton was not a village of the wealthy at that time.

By the 18th century, craftsmen such as the tailor, blacksmith, carpenter, the carter and the thatcher appear in the village indicating that the farmland was now more productive and could support more people.

It is in this time that the Old Rectory was built by Edmund Halfhyde, Rector of Girton.

In the second half of the 19th century Girton began to change more quickly. The Agricultural and Industrial Revolutions have altered the nature of village society. Familiar crafts and occupations disappeared – no blacksmith appears in the registers after 1865; no thatcher after 1881 and no horse dealer after 1863. The agricultural labourers provided the backbone of the village work, but in 1899 we hear of a shunter and an engine driver.

In the early part of the 19th century a Dame School was held in a cottage in the High Street, but in 1844 a school was built next to the church by Miss Anne Marcia Cotton (later Mrs Richard Houblon), the daughter of the rector at that time, who also gave an endowment of £1,000 to pay for its upkeep and the schoolmaster's salary. The school was to be mixed. The school became State aided in 1877 against Miss Cotton's wishes.

Girton College bought a 16 acre site at the corner of Girton Road and Huntingdon Road in 1871. The new college provided accommodation for 21 students, 3 lecture rooms and a small dining hall. The first 15 students moved in during September 1873. The college was a source of employment for the village girls either in the laundry or kitchen.

Girton Feast Week (recently revived) was held during the week after Trinity. Treats included roundabouts, and swing boats, stalls with brandy snaps etc. Nowadays there is also a fete, produce and handicraft show, pram race, disco and concerts. Not only has the Feast recently been revived but also the village or church orchestra. It plays for occasional services and Festivals.

In 1911 the population was still only 543. In 1921 it began to grow and was 1,112 by 1931. By 1948 the population had reached 2,139, following a great expanse of house building.

Girton, like many other villages, took its quota of evacuees during the first weeks of the Second World War. Tales of the exploits of these children include a cow being shot by a bow and arrow while 'jungle warfare' was being practised; also of the boy who stole a cattle drinking trough and successfully navigated it nearly as far as Waterbeach. A family of seven sisters demanded to be billeted together. A case of scarlet fever caused a whole family to be billeted in the Isolation Hospital on the Oakington Road but who all disappeared during the first night back to London and civilization.

The women of Girton did their 'bit' for the war. The WI made 4 tons of jam with fruit and sugar and preserved in cans, and the salvage campaign encouraged them:- 'Women of Girton – lay your bones here'. After the war more peaceful pursuits returned and the land opposite the church was secured and developed as a Memorial Garden to Alice Hibbert-Ware, a distinguished naturalist who lived at 'Hilary' until her death in 1944.

By 1970 there were over 3,000 on the electoral roll. There is an Animal Research Station on the Huntingdon Road and a thriving deep freeze industry behind the redundant laundry.

The City Northern Bypass, built in 1978/79 has cut through the village near Pepys Way but is in a deep cutting and has become part of the village scene, although, perhaps not a welcome one. In fact, even with the increase in house building, traffic etc., Girton has managed to keep its village qualities.

Glinton 🪶

Glinton is situated six miles north east of Peterborough, just off the A15. It is a pleasant rural community with some attractive cottages and houses built from Barnack ragstone.

The most striking feature is the lovely parish church of St Benedict with its graceful 15th century spire, a landmark for many miles around. The church itself was originally a chapel of ease to the parish of Peakirk. The 12th century Lady Chapel was once used as the village school. John Clare, the early 19th century poet from Helpston, attended here and declared his love for Mary Joyce by carving her initials on the external stonework of the east wall. The gargoyles are a prominent feature of the church. One cannot fail to notice that of those on the south side, three show faces and the fourth the opposite. The story is told that when the mason failed to obtain his remuneration he completed the work in an appropriate manner!

Opposite the church is the primary school, founded in 1845. The original building with its high pitched roof and adjoining schoolhouse have been extended over the years. The school is an important contributor to the community life of the village.

Glinton at present has three public houses and three general stores, plus a butcher's shop. The shop in Rectory Lane once housed the village fire engine, convenient to the village pump, once the major source of water. The pump was in use until the Second World War. Many a child's task on returning from school each afternoon was to take buckets to the pump and collect the family's daily water requirements.

North Fen Lane includes some lovely old houses and leads to open fields. Many older villagers mourn the loss of leafy lanes, but there are still pleasant walks to be enjoyed by today's inhabitants. The stone bridge half a mile onwards is a natural resting place and was once the illicit meeting place for John Clare and Mary Joyce.

From here can be seen the spires of several neighbouring churches across the fields.

Returning to the village, the imposing Manor Farm house betrays Dutch influence. Mary Joyce lived here and, forbidden to marry the 'lowly' John Clare, her ghost is rumoured to have been sighted at the Manor Farm's round window. There is also a legend of an underground passage running from Manor Farm to Peakirk but this has never been substantiated.

The Gransdens

Great and Little Gransden are only a few hundred yards apart and the churches of both can be seen from The Dole field which separates the villages.

Many changes have been seen over the years. Before the Second World War it was predominantly a farming community but wartime brought the Gransden Lodge airfield and the many people involved there and also evacuees. Some of these people stayed in the village after the war but the community became less agricultural with the advent of more farm machinery. The farmers are still here but are now joined by workers from the growing modern technology industry in Cambridge and the surrounding area. The village of Great Gransden also has small industrial areas on the outskirts.

Great Gransden still has its village school, Barnabas Oley Church of England Primary. This was started by the Royalist vicar of the same name in 1670 and has continued ever since at various sites in the village. It is reputed to be about the oldest primary school in the country and now boasts new buildings attached to the earlier Victorian one.

The Reading Room was created by Theodore Vincent Webb in 1871. He was also responsible for the building of the Victorian school. Today the attractive thatched reading room holds the meetings of many of the thriving groups and societies in the village. Little Gransden, although a smaller village, has a larger village hall which is used for bigger functions and sports.

The village is lucky enough to have a village stores and post office where you can still buy Zebrite black-leading alongside the more modern necessities of life like Taco Shells and Smokey Bacon crisps!

The villages have many thatched properties, some with interesting histories, but over recent years these have new neighbours in modern properties. The influx of people into the villages has brought the population back to that of earlier this century and helps the village to thrive, but everyone hopes that the villages will not grow too much and lose their character.

Grantchester 🦢

The parish is bounded on two sides by water. To the south is the Bourn Brook, running from the west to Byron's Pool. At Byron's Pool, also called Old Mills, the brook joins the river Cam also called the Granta and Rhee or Rea. This river is the parish's eastern boundary down to Newnham.

The history of the river is nearly all the history of its mills. In the Domesday Book two mills are mentioned and it is possible there was one at Byron's Pool and another at Newnham. They were both worth 40 shillings and 'half a wier half a thousand eels'. It was said the best time for catching eels was after a thunderstorm when the river was full and muddy. One man is supposed to have sold enough eels to buy his granddaughter a grand piano! There is no mill in Grantchester now, the last one was destroyed by fire on 30th October 1928.

The parish church of St Andrew and St Mary stands on a slight rise in the middle of the village. It is in the living of Corpus Christi College, Cambridge. It consists of a 14th century chancel and a 15th century tower and nave. When a south aisle was added in 1875, remains of what are believed to have been Saxon grave-covers were found, which point to the very early existence of a church upon this site. The bowl of the font would appear to be Norman. It is made of Purbeck stone and is very large, 30 inches in diameter. Both its size and simple form give an indication of its early date. During repairs in 1875, a doorway was discovered in the north wall of the nave.

The village has been made world famous by Rupert Brooke and his poem, *The Old Vicarage Grantchester*. The present owner of the Old Vicarage is Jeffrey Archer the author and politician. Grantchester must be the only village in the rather unusual position of having three vicarages. The first was the Old Vicarage, the second situated in Vicarage Drive is now a private home called

Glebe House and the third is next to the church where the present vicar lives.

Every second Sunday in the month snacks are served at Byron's Lodge. Home made food is prepared and served by voluntary help and the profit is given to the vicar to spend at his discretion. It is organised by Ivor and June Slater, who incidentally have won the Dunmow Flitch.

Great Paxton 🦋

Situated three miles to the north of the market town of St Neots, Great Paxton is approached over a hill with pleasant sweeping views of the river Ouse and Ouse valley.

The village today has changed from thatched cottages, a small council estate and surrounding farms, to a large village of over 300 houses. There is a small school, shop and post office, and a pub called The Bell. There was another pub called The Black Bull, but this was converted to a house. Other additions to the village include the recreation ground where local football and cricket teams play, and the children's play area.

At the top of Paxton Hill there is a vineyard, and the grapes are made into a fine white wine called 'Paxton Crest'.

The church, the Minster Church of the Holy Trinity stands out as a remarkable building dating back to about 1020 AD. It is specifically mentioned in the Domesday Book, and is said to be one of the oldest in England. The outside is seen as mostly 15th century but once inside one sees the imposing Saxon church, with its pillars and arches opening onto the aisle, quite unlike anything existing in England but similar to types found on the Continent.

The river Ouse runs to the west of the village, and it is very pleasant to walk along its banks to the cornmill at Offord, or there is a small nature reserve on the edge of the village towards Offord D'Arcy called 'Bankside'.

Great Shelford 🦋

'Folks in Shelford and those parts
Have twisted lips and twisted hearts'

These malicious words by Rupert Brooke have brought fame to Shelford throughout the world but few people know exactly where it is! It lies on the A130, south of Cambridge. Shelford was first mentioned in the 11th century under the name of Scelford (shallow ford). In 1279 there were about 105 houses and 38 landholders.

The common land in Great Shelford was enclosed in 1835 after which 64% of the land belonged to Gonville and Caius, St John's and Jesus Colleges. The remainder was divided among smaller owners.

In 1845 the railway to Cambridge was opened and Shelford had its own station. The railway led to more building which still continues. The M11 motorway was opened in 1980 with an access less than one mile from the village.

The population of Shelford is mainly professional, some working in local small firms. Torch Computers Ltd is housed at Abberley House built in 1870. The village has excellent shopping and parking facilities. It has its own Health Care Centre and there are many community and social organisations.

The church of St Mary was largely rebuilt about 1400 but includes features from the 12th, 13th and 14th centuries. The spire was blown down in 1703 and was restored in 1843, 1931 and 1985. There is a Doom painting of about 1400 on the chancel arch. The chancel screen is 15th century. The parish register survives from 1557. There is a very active Baptist chapel in High Street.

Little Shelford shares the Church of England primary school which is a modern building. The old school building is now a garage but it is said that there were many 'brainy' schoolchildren in Great Shelford during the last century. The University Dons were not allowed girl friends within four miles of their colleges. Great Shelford is exactly four miles!

Several very interesting old houses are to be found in Shelford. Several are thatched and one in Church Street may have been a guildhall in the early 16th century. There are four public houses. All have a good history and all have a brisk trade!

Great Staughton

Surrounded on three sides by farmland and on the fourth by moors, Great Staughton was an insignificant sleepy village which has evolved since the 1970s into an active, small village – a good blend of past and present – boasting a beautiful 800 year old church, a highly thought of primary school, three shops, post office, two nurseries, three pubs and a well-used village hall.

It sits either side of a small stretch of the A45 in Cambridge-shire, half a mile from the Bedfordshire border. The village would not be on any tourist route, for it would not merit the adjective 'beautiful', but in spring, when all the daffodils are gently waving in full bloom along the green verges, many a motorist has paused to take a photograph, and this heralding of spring helps offset the nuisance of container lorries noisily trundling through on their way to the Midlands or the East coast.

A stranger to the village would wonder what the inhabitants were like, but would not be long in doubt, as it is a very friendly, caring and thriving community with over 25 associations and clubs to cater for all ages and tastes. Each of its 350 households receives an informative, voluntarily produced magazine each month, including reports from various meetings, events etc and giving a diary of forthcoming activities.

Great Wilbraham

Great Wilbraham was an important place in early times, situated as it was on a narrow belt of firm land between marshes and dense forest, through which the Romans launched their attack on Boadi-cea and later, in the 7th century King Penda's Midland Federation marched against East Anglia. The great earthwork, Fleam Dyke, is a reminder of these stirring times. The victorious Penda bestowed the land behind the dyke on his daughter, Wilburh and she, in turn, gave her name to the village: Wilburgaham – 'Wilburh's homestead'.

One of the oldest tracks in England, the Streetway, passes through the parish and excavations in the area have revealed evidence that there was a Roman settlement there before Wilburh's time.

In the 13th century the manor of Great Wilbraham was acquired by the Knights Templar. In the 14th century the Templars fell into disgrace and the Wilbraham manor passed to their rivals, the Knights Hospitallers. The house on the site of the preceptory is known as the Temple to this day and one of its out-buildings,

The Dovecote at Great Wilbraham

dating from the 15th century, was probably part of the private apartments of a commander of the Hospitallers.

After Henry VIII's suppression of religious orders Great Wilbraham had a measure of independence under absentee landlords and the village was run by its leading farming families, the Olivers, the Ballards and the Smiths. Perhaps it was this independent spirit which made Great Wilbraham a centre of nonconformity in the 17th century. Behind Crossways (originally Cross Farm) in the High Street is a small nonconformist graveyard where members of the Webb, Paul and Dennis families are buried.

The last decades of the 18th century saw great changes in the village when the Hicks family moved into the Temple and bought up much of the farmland. The poor had the present common on which they could graze one cow or two yearling calves. Many householders in the village still enjoy these common rights.

The Hicks family took a great interest in the welfare of the villagers. Most of the cottages belonged to their estate and most of the men worked on the land, so life revolved around the 'Big

House'. Under the spell of this vigorous paternalism Great Wilbraham remained out of the modern world until the Second World War when an American airfield was built nearby and tanks were stationed in the Temple park. Even in the early 1960s most of the older inhabitants of the village worked on the land and a newspaper article of the time records that 'the whole rhythm of village life is dependent on the harvest and the sowing'.

It was the advent of mains drainage in the early 1970s which really opened the village up to new building, but luckily only 'infilling' has been allowed and on the whole the new houses blend harmoniously with the old cottages and the village remains a close and friendly community.

Guilden Morden 🌿

Guilden Morden, once described as Golden Morden, lies in pleasantly undulating country southwest of Cambridge, near the Bedfordshire border and close to Hertfordshire. It was mentioned in the Domesday Book as the 'other' Morden – alia Mordun – to differentiate it from its close neighbour, Steeple Morden which at the time was slightly less populous.

In 1871 there were a little over 1000 people living in the village, the last increase resulting from the prosperity which came to Guilden Morden with the digging of coprolites. This was a phosphate dug as an early fertiliser but the industry died with imports from Chile. Consequently the population fell and in 1931, 60 years later, the population had dropped to 533. Now this quiet village is once again becoming a sought-after place in which to live.

In common with most local villages there were a large number of public houses from the 19th century. Though there are only two remaining open, the Edward VII in Trap Road and The Three Tuns in the High Street, many older residents can still name at least nine. They can also recall a butcher's shop, two bakeries, the last one, Lindsay's closing in 1976 and they also remember small grocer's and sweet shops. Now the village has a general store and post office.

Until the mid 1970s, Guilden Morden was one of the only villages in the district to have a farrier. When Mr Oswald Kaye died the forge closed and the name plate on a house in Church Street indicates where the last forge was.

No story about Guilden Morden would be complete without a mention of St Mary's church built on the highest point in the village with a splendid tower and lofty spire, a feature of the neighbourhood. St Mary's church began in the 13th century and was in its present form by the 15th, though according to history there was certainly a church of some kind there soon after the Norman Conquest. There has also been a suggestion that it was all built on an earlier religious site.

Other notable features of the church are the parclose or rood screen and the church clock. The screen has survived intact, and research into church woodwork indicates that of its date it is the finest of its kind in the country. According to records the clock, with no minute hand, is said to be one of the best preserved of tower clocks in the neighbourhood.

There has been an Independent, Congregational chapel in the village for about a century and a half. There was indeed mention of the Presbyterians in the early 18th century. The handsome building in Pound Green was closely associated with the Rev Joseph Stockbridge who founded it and continued as its pastor for 50 years.

The village is proud of its modern Church of England primary school in Pound Green where there are 67 pupils. The school was officially opened by the Bishop of Ely in 1975, though the children moved from the old school in Church Street in 1974. The old school built in 1846 is now a private residence.

There are a lot of old houses and cottages in Guilden Morden, a few of them thatched. Among the older properties is the fine manor house of Morden Hall in Trap Road. It stands on a moated site and has its own chapel. On Avenells in Church Street is the date 1680 but the house has been restored and enlarged over the years.

Haddenham

Haddenham is the highest and the most southern village in the Isle of Ely. As the village is 116 feet above sea level and is surrounded by the low lying fens it is a very noticeable feature of the land-scape.

Holy Trinity Church, Haddenham

Because of its position, Haddenham was a well-known settlement long before the fens were drained. Ovin, who was steward to Queen Etheldreda, founded a Saxon church here in 673 AD.

During recent years excavations in the fen at Hillrow have unearthed a Roman settlement and a Neolithic megalith in a long barrow. As the latter is the first, and at the moment the only, wooden mortuary structure to be found intact, the 6000 year old mausoleum is a particularly exciting find. The mausoleum, which is 6 metres long and 1½ metres wide will be housed in the British Museum, but it is hoped that a replica will be contructed in Haddenham.

On the site of the one-time Haddenham Gas Company, brick-yard and pits, is now an established lake, naturalised garden and wildlife sanctuary. It is hoped that this important conservation area, covering some five acres, will shortly come into the ownership of the Parish Council, to ensure its preservation.

The village has several old houses and at the top of the hill, the Holy Trinity church, with its medieval kingpost roof and a fine 15th century font. The church is a delightful setting for many occasions, but, perhaps, particularly for the 'Flowers and Paintings' weekend, held each July.

Next to the church is the Arkenstall Village Centre, so named because it was previously the school, founded by Robert Arkenstall in 1723 and named after him.

In the High Street is the Farmland Museum, started by a schoolboy and run by the Delanoy family it has a growing collection of agricultural implements and local bygones. The museum also encourages 'live' exhibits of craftspeople working on country crafts.

Still travelling south, visitors leave the village, passing the spot where Ovin's Cross stood before being taken to Ely Cathedral. In about ¼ mile is the recently found Quaker burial ground and the remains of the last of the village's windmills. On the right is a red brick house which is unusual in as much as the bricks used in its construction were baked on the site.

And so to Aldreth, a small hamlet with a Baptist chapel and the English Provender factory. Here the houses run right to the edge of the fens and only farm roads continue from the village. Here the waters of the 1947 floods lapped dangerously close.

If travellers approach the village from the west they will be immediately aware of North Hill which gives some of the finest views of the fens. This is Hillrow and has a terrace of houses built to accommodate Dutch drainage workers. These men were most unpopular locally as by draining the fens they totally altered the lifestyle of the fen people, whose livelihood was founded on fishing and wildfowling. The same Dutch engineers are believed to have built the oldest house in Haddenham, the Porch House, which has 1657 inscribed over the front porch.

Approaching the village centre visitors pass the village green with its fine, locally crafted village sign and bordered by the manor house and the Baptist chapel on one side and the Old Baptist Hall and burial ground on the other, the latter to become a new Health Centre and children's play area respectively.

Hardwick 🌿

The village of Hardwick is situated about five miles west of Cambridge, just north of the ancient track called 'Portway' and is the nucleus of a parish of 1438 acres. The earliest written record of Hardwick dates from AD 991 when the manor of Hardwick was given to the monks of Ely by the chieftain Brithnoth or Beorhtnoth in recognition of the hospitality his army received when marching into Essex to fight the Danes. It is accepted that the name Hardwick originates from the old English 'herd' meaning herd or flock and 'wic' meaning dwelling or village and that Hardwick was originally an outlying shepherds' settlement subordinate to Toft. The soil is heavy boulder clay and despite the origins of its name, the land around Hardwick has generally been and still is more suited to arable farming than the keeping of livestock.

The See of Ely was created in 1109 and the manor of Hardwick was eventually converted for the Bishop's use. Bishop Matthew Wren, uncle of Sir Christopher Wren finally endowed the manor of Hardwick to Pembroke College, Cambridge to enable its newly completed chapel, designed by his nephew, to be kept in good repair.

The small parish church of St Mary is a simple building consisting of nave, chancel, west tower with spire, small porch and modern vestry. It is built of field stones in the Perpendicular style dating from the late 14th or 15th century. However, a Decorated window on the south side of the chancel indicates an earlier stone building. In fact there is a reference to a church at Hardwick dated 1217. In 1858 medieval mural drawings were discovered on the south wall of the church, some of which have recently been re-exposed. The relatively complete registers date from 1569. Records frequently refer to the poor state of repair of the church. For example in 1836 the numerous holes in the roof provided ventilation but also admitted sparrows to the services! The interior of the church is currently undergoing restoration by members of the congregation. Since 1966 the rector of Hardwick has also served the parishes of Toft and Caldecote.

There is a record of a dame school at Hardwick in 1789. However, following the Elementary Education Act of 1870 a new schoolroom and schoolhouse was built which opened in 1872. This was sited on glebe land near the church and cost £452, financed largely by private subscription. This school was closed in 1968 and for a few years there was no school in Hardwick. However, to meet the needs of a rapidly expanding population, a new Community Primary School was opened in 1979.

For centuries Hardwick was a totally agricultural community centred around the church and village green, with a small population fluctuating with the prosperity of farming on the relatively infertile soil. Since 1900 the village has gradually changed. The village smithy and bakehouse have gone and in the 1930s and 1940s several houses were built along the Cambridge to St Neots road about half a mile from the centre of the village. From 1970, however, several hundred houses have been built so that the parish now has about 890 households with a population of 2240. There is a public house, two shops and post office and several small businesses. Consequently, although the village is still completely surrounded by farmland, apple orchards and woodland, it is now very much a dormitory village for Cambridge.

Harston

Harston lies some five miles from Cambridge, in the valley of the Cam or Rhee. The name of the village has evolved from different spellings, the closest to present day usage being Hares-town; this and surrounding villages eg Fox-town and Hawkes-town, are said to have been the hunting ground of Queen Elizabeth I. There is evidence to suggest that Harston is of Saxon origin, but Roman, as well as Saxon pottery has been found.

The village is situated on the busy A10 road. It has been said that Harston 'is one long street', but with recent building developments this is now less so. The 'long street' was always bustling with travellers from Cambridge to London in wagons, carts and coaches and the inns catered for passengers and traders of all kinds. One of the oldest inns, the Coach (or Wagon) and Horses is possibly a 16th century house, and was recorded in 1800. It has been practically re-built, and is now a private dwelling.

At the entrance to the village, approached from Cambridge, on the High Street, stands a public house The Old English Gentleman, newly built in 1839 and named for the then rector of Fowlmere: at the opposite end of the street, where stands the war memorial, is the Pemberton Arms built c1865. In between these two points the present day traveller will find the village stores and post office, an antique shop, garages, car showrooms etc, replacing among other things the wheelwright's shop, and the smithy.

The manor house is of 17th century origin, but was extensively remodelled in the 18th and 19th centuries. Beside the manor is the parish church of All Saints. The building, built of field stones and ashlar dressing is mostly mid to late 14th century, but there is some evidence of an earlier church on the site. The church was restored in 1853. The wooden pulpit is an example of medieval craftsmanship: the octagonal font is 15th century.

Turning on to the road to Haslingfield and bearing left, we

come to a popular riverside walk. It was here in 1645 that a force of King Charles' cavalry attempted to fight their way across the river Rhee. A bloody battle ensued and the crossing was held by Cromwell's men. The site is known as The Red Field. The watermill in the vicinity dates from 1086. In the 1960s it was bought by an animal feed company and it has now undergone an architectural award-winning transformation to become the headquarters of a scientific company.

Winding north from the church is Button End, a narrow lane, partly residential, partly industrial. In 1870 it was the site of the digging of coprolites, involving an influx of 55 immigrant workers.

The village sign is situated on the (now diminished) green. It depicts a rook, a honey skip and water springs, the latter recalling the beautiful clear water which welled up at many points in the village, to be collected by the people.

Hartford ༄

The earliest settlement in this stretch of the river Ouse was Hartford – older than nearby Huntingdon and Godmanchester. The Saxons called it Hereforde meaning 'army ford', and it is recorded under this name in the Domesday Book. The village was originally along the banks of the river which was the main form of transport, but now it has expanded to the north and west linking up with the Borough of Huntingdon.

Church Lane leads to the church and river. The cottage which stands facing the river was originally the Anchor Inn and in 1275 a waterwheel was constructed there. Nearby in the meadow in the 13th century, St Giles' Hospital was built.

The parish church of All Saints, over 800 years old, is built on the north bank of the river, surrounded by a well maintained churchyard with colourful flower beds overlooking peaceful meadows. This picturesque setting inspires not only local couples, but many outside the parish, to wed in the church. A family of inquisitive swans are often part of the wedding photographs.

About a mile further downstream lies the Hartford Marina full of luxury craft for those wishing to enjoy a holiday afloat. Formerly a series of gravel pits, it now has direct access to the river by a purpose-built channel, and was given an award by ARC for its pleasing landscape transformation.

Returning to the village and wishing to quench your thirst, what better way than with a refreshing pint at one of the two local hostelries. The King of the Belgians (formerly King of the Prussians) is situated in that part of Main Street which happily is now by-passed by Longstaff Way and the roar of today's traffic. In 1964 workmen digging near The King of the Belgians public house unearthed a hoard of 1108 French and English coins dated between 1450 and 1503. The silver coins, many in mint condition, were removed to the British Museum. A little more modern in age is the Barley Mow, with a mansard roof, built around 1804 with masonry from the remains of St Benet's church in Huntingdon.

Hartford House was built in 1730. This is a red brick house and was held in 1822 by Richard Bateman. The great features of the house are the 1730 curved staircase and the panelling in the hall and dining room. The grounds go down to the river. The manor house opposite is half-timbered, built probably by Robert Taylor, lord of the manor who died in 1608.

A shopping parade serves the more recently developed part of the village and includes a supermarket, post office, fruit and vegetable shop, newsagent and fish and chip shop. Nearby are situated the infant and junior schools, built over 20 years ago for the rising population, whose pupils move on to comprehensive schools in Huntingdon. In the older part of the village is another small grocery store and hairdressing salon. The social centre of the community is the village hall where numerous activities take place.

With the ever increasing traffic in East Anglia, a northern by-pass cutting through agricultural land to the east of the village should help to relieve the heavy congestion in the region, where many are employed in the new expanding light industries. There are plans for further housing development in this area.

Hauxton 🌿

Visitors to Hauxton may well think that it is a comparatively new village with an ever-expanding factory at one end and new housing estates at the other. However, nothing could be further from the truth. The Beaker Folk, Bronze Age people settled in the area by the present-day mill, where the river Cam could be forded. It is probable that there has been a mill there since Roman times, and the mill at 'Havochestun' was certainly mentioned in the Domesday

Book. Over the centuries the nearby farmers brought their corn there to be ground, but the mill's heyday was in the late 18th century when it was also used for crushing coleseed (rape) for oil. In addition, the managers traded in corn, coal, pitch and tar, and brick and timber for building. At that time six passenger coaches a day plied between Cambridge and London and would stop at the two alehouses, The Ship and The Chequers, close by the mill.

Following a disastrous fire in 1851, the present mill was built. It continued to grind corn until 1974 when the last miller, Mr Maurice Turner, retired. It then passed into the hands of the nearby agrochemical factory and, sadly, now stands idle. The Old Mill House, a handsome Georgian house, and the new Mill House, built early this century, are no longer lived in and the old Mill Farmhouse and cottages have been demolished to make way for the expansion of the factory.

The parish church of St Edmund also has an ancient history. The present building was erected in the early 12th century and it is believed that a little wooden church stood on the site for about 150 years before that. So, in 1969, the village celebrated the church's millenium with a week of special services, concerts and plays, culminating in a pageant depicting the history of the church.

In 1870, led by the then vicar, the people of Hauxton were able to provide a school for the children. This handsome building served the community for over a century until, in 1971, the school was threatened with closure. The villagers strongly opposed this proposal and, instead, a new school was built and the village was able to purchase the old school building. Following alterations, it re-opened in 1977 – Jubilee Year – as the village hall.

During the First World War some local men were employed in digging for coprolites – fossilised dinosaur droppings! – which made excellent fertiliser.

Before the Second World War many of the men of Hauxton worked on the land but, with the changes in farming which have taken place over the past 50 years, very few do so now.

In the 1950s people passing through the village might have seen a young bull from the local farm being taken for a walk along Church Road. On Sunday mornings he was taken for his weekly treat – half a pint at the King's Head!

Helpston ✌

Helpston is situated on the edge of the fens, about seven miles north west of Peterborough, with a population of about 800.

It is an attractive village with a large number of old buildings constructed of the local grey stone with collyweston roofs. The attractiveness of the centre of the village has been recognised by its designation as a Conservation Area. It has a long history dating back at least as far as the 12th century, although there are no records of it in the Domesday Book. The Butter Cross at the core of the village is 14th century. Its heart-shaped base is supposed to represent the Heart of Christ and a market was held there during the 16th and 17th centuries.

Helpston is most widely known as the birthplace of John Clare, the so-called 'Peasant Poet' who lived from 1793 to 1864. The primary school is named after him and there is a John Clare memorial, dated 1869, at the village centre.

Few people work in the village, most going to Stamford, Peterborough or, indeed, London. However there are several farming families who still work the surrounding land. The paper mills which were founded in the 19th century employed 230 people in 1978, but the numbers have now dropped considerably.

Hemingford Abbots ✌

Hemingford Abbots is a small, picturesque riverside village dating back to AD 974, with a population of around 600. It is situated just off the A604 between the historic market towns of Huntingdon and St Ives.

The lovely church of St Margaret of Antioch is well preserved and maintained, parts of it dating back to the 12th century. There are many desirable properties in the village, a number of which are thatched, and countless beautiful gardens. The attractive Axe and Compass pub occupies a prominent position in the centre of the village.

The well kept village hall was judged 1st in the Best Kept Village Hall competition in 1974 and 1985 – bearing in mind that it was formerly a First World War Army hut! Although the Peace Memorial Playing Fields are situated just over the border into

Hemingford Grey they are jointly owned and administered by both Hemingfords and are, as the name implies, a lasting memorial to those villagers who gave their lives in both World Wars.

The annual Regatta is combined with Hemingford Grey and remains the only amateur regatta in the country today.

A popular walk with residents is across the meadows to Houghton and, if desired, one can continue on through the Thicket to St Ives. Hemingford Grey is but a short distance away, making a very pleasant riverside walk and a favourite rendezvous for fishermen and the small children who love to feed the ducks and swans and admire the large numbers of Brent geese which winter on the meadows beyond. Although the days of point-to-point races on the Common – at the far end of Common Lane – have long since past (due to the excavation of sand and gravel) it is still possible to walk to Godmanchester via this route.

Hemingford Grey 🪶

This delightful rural village lies one and a half miles to the south west of St Ives, on the banks of the river Ouse. Owned originally by Ramsey Abbey in 1041, the village and lands of 'Hemmingforde' eventually passed into the ownership of Reginald de Grey and his successors, and thereafter from the 14th century was known as Hemingford Grey.

The village has many picturesque and historic buildings, the most interesting of these being the original old manor house. Originally a stone Norman hall, built by Payn de Hemingford in the 12th century, it has since had many additions in varying styles. The original moat surrounds the house on three sides, with attractive gardens stretching to the river bank on the fourth. Believed to be the oldest inhabited house in England, it is presently occupied by the famous children's authoress Lucy M. Boston.

The High Street, which is in the heart of the village, offers an interesting variety of period buildings, from Glebe Cottage, a timber framed thatched cottage dating from 1583, to the attractive yellow brick River House, which was built in the late 18th century.

Also situated in the High Street, are the three small shops, the village post office, a pottery, the church rooms, and the recently restored reading rooms, outside which stands the seat commemorating the award for Best Kept Village in 1986. Last but not least comes the Cock Inn which has served the villagers since 1767.

At the end of the High Street lies the river, and the River Walk, which affords the most delightful views across green meadowland towards Houghton, and the distant spires of St Ives' and Hemingford Abbots' churches. Standing on the riverbank at the bend in the river, is the attractive 12th century St James's church, presenting one of the most beautiful and tranquil scenes to be found in the area. Adjacent to the church is Hemingford Grey House, built in 1697. Once the rectory, it is now a conference centre.

For the keen naturalists and bird watchers, there is the Marsh Lane Walk Society, a group which was formed at the instigation of the Parish Council, to conserve and improve the reclaimed gravel pits on the southern boundary of the village. After much hard work by the Society, and co-operation from Redlands, the gravel pit owners, this area now forms an attractive lake, with pleasant perimeter walk. It is renowned for the many resident and migratory wildfowl and birds which make use of the natural habitat.

An annual event worthy of note is the Hemingford Regatta, which while not as famous as Henley, is nevertheless a very popular and pleasurable day out. It has been held on this stretch of the river since 1909, and is believed to be the last event of this kind in the country to still use ordinary pleasure boats rather than racing craft.

Hildersham 🦡

Hildersham is an attractive unspoilt village on the banks of the Granta (which becomes the Cam) lying about nine miles southeast of Cambridge, with a population of some 200.

Hildersham was also once a Roman camp, one of many between Colchester and the North. The meadow behind the church, known as Dovehouse Meadow, has yielded Roman coins and pottery, and exposed Roman foundations.

Hildersham may have been founded by Hildric, but today it owes its beautiful wooded appearance to a Victorian family, the Goodwins, who endowed both the village and the church with many treasures. Magnificent beech trees surround the parish, especially to the south of the river, whilst the Austrian pines,

The skeleton brass in Hildersham Church

mainly north of the river, were brought in by the Reverend Goodwin, and were at that time a rarity. They are now about 150 years old, but sadly many of them, especially the beeches were lost in the violent storm of October 1987.

Hildersham is notable as being the last village in England in which the medieval system of stripfields was abolished, and the common lands enclosed in the year 1886, some 150 years after the first Act of Enclosure. A further event occurred in 1886 – the iron bridge over the Granta in the middle of the village was built by the local blacksmith, commissioned by the Goodwin family. In fact, the blacksmith's shop remained open until 1940 on Forge Green (opposite The Pear Tree Inn) where a plaque now stands to mark its position. The Goodwins also straightened the river, and if you stand on the bridge you can make out the course of the original river to the east and the west – always the first parts to flood!

Hildersham has a large area of common land, some of which is used by local farmers, but most is available to villagers and visitors just to enjoy, which is one of Hildersham's greatest assets.

Hildersham's church, The Holy Trinity, was founded in 1150. The oldest surviving portions – the vaulted sacristy and western tower – date from the early 13th century. The church has many special features and there are some well-known brasses in the floor of the chancel aisle, including three of the Paris family who provided the best Latin chronicler of the 13th century in the name of Matthew Paris. The fourth brass is of a shroud skeleton of a man which dates from 1530. Close observers will note that there is a keyhole shape cut into this brass which dates from the time it was hung on the church door to frighten away body-snatchers (or so the story goes!).

The church is very rare inasmuch as the whole interior of the chancel, including roof, walls, window frames and mullions was decorated in 1890 with stencilled floral work and painted panels depicting scenes from the Bible. It was all commissioned by the Goodwin family who also provided two rectors, father and son, for 94 years from 1806 to 1900.

Other notable buildings in the village include 'Mabbutts', the oldest surviving house, which is timber framed with overhangs, and was built in the very early 16th century. The watermill stands on a cut to the east of the village and straddles the boundary with Linton. The windmill, built in a field to the south of the watermill in 1837 has been without its sails for many years.

During renovation of Burford House, a farmhouse previously believed to be from the late 17th century, some murals were uncovered from Cromwellian days depicting distinct Royalist tendencies by the owners. These are being restored, as they have lain hidden behind panelling and other decorations for about 350 years.

Hilton

The parish of Hilton lies on the edge of the fens on slightly higher ground, as the name suggests. The village is surrounded by fields that are cultivated for cereal crops and the vivid yellow flowering oil-seed rape.

Old and new houses with generous gardens are set around the green and along the streets. Shady paths lead over white painted footbridges crossing the ditches that drain the land. The water collects in weed covered ponds over which ancient willows drape their branches. At one point the water crosses the road making the ford quite deep in rainy weather.

The old farmhouses such as Manor Farm, College Farm, Cross Farm and Oaktree Farm tell of the once rural occupation. Now nearly all land is farmed collectively by commercial firms.

From the 85 houses and 535 population in 1881 the village has grown to 340 houses and over 1000 population. People of all walks of life reside here now. Fortunately there are some who have lived in the village all their life and can recall the past when village life was self sufficient with a butcher, a baker, two general stores, a carpenter, a blacksmith and four public houses. Today only one general store, the post office and the Prince of Wales pub remain. A garage and motor repair shop serves the needs of modern day transport.

Many visitors are attracted by the picturesque village green with its maze dating back to 1660. It is one of only eight surviving turf mazes in England. The monument in the centre commemorates William Sparrow who created the maze.

The green is all that remains of the once extensive common land villagers used for grazing cattle. Even today the right to pasture 15 cows is still attached to some properties. Alas, no cows can be seen today. They have given place to the cricket ground and the football field. 'Capability' Brown, famous for his landscape gardening, may have had a hand in the layout of Hilton Green, as he was at one time lord of the manor of Fenstanton and Hilton. In spite of having lost the elms and large beeches there are still a great number of magnificent trees to be seen. The walnut trees planted in the 1950s by Richard Garnet are enjoyed especially in autumn when the nuts are ripe.

The old village school was closed in 1955 after over 100 years of use and the children travel by bus to Fenstanton. After restoration the picturesque building has found a new purpose as the village hall and is again a central feature of village life.

Standing on the highest point, surrounded by the walled graveyard and old trees is the church of St Mary Magdalene. Although mostly dating from the 14th and 15th century, parts go back to the 12th century. There is a peal of six bells – the latest two were dedicated in December 1987. Not far from it is the Methodist church which was built in 1867.

Hilton is a friendly and welcoming village with an active community life. This is clearly evident in the revival of the celebration of Feast Week commemorating the Feast of St Mary Magdalene which falls on 22nd July.

Hinxton 🦢

This village was once Henchistone, then Hyngeston and today Hinxton. Some 70 years ago there existed two general grocery shops, a butcher's shop, post office, dairy, two public houses, the parish church, a chapel, village school, four farms, plus one or two smallholdings. There was also a watermill, which after the Second World War became redundant and fell into poor condition. Fortunately, thanks to the Cambridge Preservation Society, this has now been completely restored and is once again in working order, being open to the public on certain days of the year. The main occupation in those days was of course agriculture.

Today there is no post office or shop of any kind, one public house and three farms. There is no school or chapel, and the church at best has one Sunday service, as the vicar is also responsible for two other parishes.

A very old custom is the distribution of charity coal, or other help with heating to the elderly folk in winter, provided by the trustees of the Ann Housden Charity. Events enjoyed in the past were the Hinxton Feast held on the 26th June, and the three village flower shows and sports held around mid July each year in rotation at Duxford, Hinxton and Ickleton.

In the parish are still some very old and interesting properties, including the Red Lion public house and the old manor house standing opposite. Church Green Cottage is another fine old building with a thatched roof, which was once four small cottages. At the north end of the village stands the Oak House, which years ago consisted of a farmhouse and two small cottages and this dwelling contains some very fine oak panelling.

In the past many of the cottages in the village were owned by the Hinxton Hall estate, one at least of which bears a wooden stag's head, a replica of the Hinxton estate crest. Legend has it that when the stag hears the church clock strike 12 midnight, it goes to the river to drink. Alas today the church clock is not in working order, while many of the former estate cottages have passed into private ownership.

Changes in the village in general have been caused by fire. We are told that on Tuesday 6th March 1743 a terrible fire occurred. It began at 11 am at the malting of Mr Burling, who burned his malt with straw inadvisedly when the wind was high. Ten houses were consumed in four hours.

Histon & Impington

Histon and Impington, lying approximately four miles north west of Cambridge, have a population of about 7000 and are almost one village in that the boundaries are intermingled. Each has its own Parish Council and so far all attempts to amalgamate have been unsuccessful.

Both villages are mentioned in the Domesday Book and Impington was recorded in an Anglo Saxon charter dated AD 907. However, there is no earlier record of Histon (the larger of the two) although there is no doubt that a settlement existed in former times.

Mrs Elizabeth Woodcock of Impington has gone down in history as a result of having survived being buried in the snow for eight days in 1799. She had attended Cambridge market on Saturday 2nd February and on her return she was thrown (or fell) from her horse and took shelter under a hedge. The snow drifted over her until she was completely covered. Eventually she found an aperture in the snow through which she pushed a red handkerchief tied to a stick, which led to her discovery, but not until the following Sunday! She lived until July 1799 although bedridden and in very poor health.

Moses Carter, the Histon giant, was over seven feet tall and lived in the 19th century. His tall hat and one of his boots are still in existence and schoolchildren are delighted when they are allowed to try on the hat!

Each village has a 13th century parish church and there is also one Baptist church, one Methodist church and a Salvation Army hall all with their own social activities. Spurgeon, the well known Baptist preacher, is known to have given sermons in a barn on the green.

The red brick Old House (the first brick built house in Histon) is said to be haunted and contains two priests' hiding holes. It is believed to date from the 16th century and for many years was thought to have been the oldest house. But recent discoveries indicate that the thatched Stone Corner Cottage is even older and could have been a guildhall probably dating from the 14th century.

Chivers & Sons Ltd started their jam making in a barn at Impington in 1873. This grew so much that in 1875 a factory was built near Histon station with a siding for its own use and employing some 4000 people at its peak. Messrs Chivers were extremely good employers and provided many facilities for both their own workers and the villagers; for instance in 1903 a Men's Institute was opened in the old Baptist chapel on the green which incorporated a reading room, billiards room and a gymnasium. Baths were also provided, which were quite an innovation.

Unwins Seeds Ltd is another firm which started from small beginnings and which is known throughout the country, especially for its sweet peas which were developed by the founder of the firm, Mr W.J. Unwin. People from many parts of the country visit the trial grounds during the summer.

The village green, which is in Histon, has a brook running through it on which are many ducks. It is a picturesque spot which attracts many visitors, with a large grassy area, beautiful trees and a variety of interesting houses around. The village pump still stands in its original position and it is thought that at one time there were stocks nearby.

Impington Village College was opened in 1939 as a secondary school and has been greatly added to over the years, more recently by the addition of accommodation for handicapped children. Designed by the well known architects Walter Gropius and Maxwell Fry it also included an adult centre and was built on land given by the Chivers family which was part of the Impington Hall estate. The Hall was demolished in 1953 but had at one time been occupied by Talbot Pepys who was visited there by his nephew, the diarist Samuel Pepys. The name is commemorated in one of the roads, Pepys Terrace.

Over the years both villages have grown tremendously and this is continuing as there is now 'Vision Park' in the course of construction for high tech. industrial use, offices, etc. Recent additions are the Post House hotel on the outskirts, the private Cambridge Lea Hospital in New Road, and Anglia Water Authority's newly built headquarters in Station Road.

Holme 🦙

Holme is situated on the B660 Kimbolton to East Coast road, two miles east of the A1. Although it is a small village (population 566) it has some claim to fame. Just outside the village on Holme Fen is the lowest road in England, nine to ten feet below sea level at the last measurement taken for the Guinness Book of Records.

During the last century William Wells, the squire, reclaimed the land from Whittlesey Mere by drainage. Although he unfortunately spent all the family wealth, the village is now blessed with some of the best arable land in the East of England.

In 1851 on the south west edge of Whittlesey Mere an iron post was driven into the peat flush with the surface. To this day we are still able to measure peat shrinkage by the famous Iron Post. The top is now 13 feet above the ground level. This post, reputedly from the Crystal Palace Exhibition, replaced wooden posts which had been driven in in 1848.

St Giles' church is relatively modern, built in the mid 19th century, but there has been a church on the site for many centuries. Behind the church is the oldest dwelling in the village, dating from 1770.

The squire's family lived in Holmewood Hall, rebuilt in 1873, which is now used as a field station and offices for the British Sugar Corporation, who have restored some of the rooms to their former glory. Unfortunately it is not open to the public except on very special occasions.

There are a few farm cottages built in the Gothic style popular in the 19th century. The old vicarage, built in 1859, stands in Station Road and opposite is the post office, the corner of which is rounded to enable carts to negotiate the corners of the narrow lanes more easily.

The eastern boundary of the village is the level crossing developed when the Great Northern and LNER railways built a station (unfortunately closed in the 1960s). There was also a branch line to Ramsey and a wharf where farm produce was offloaded from horse-drawn barges, which were then re-loaded with coal for the pumping engines on the fens.

Holywell-cum-Needingworth 🦢

Holywell-cum-Needingworth is a village which is situated on the river Ouse about two miles from the historic market town of St Ives. The name of Holywell was given to the district around the well in the churchyard many years before the growth of the hamlet of Needingworth. Some authorities think that the name Holywell arose in Roman times from the use made of the well for holy purposes.

The church of St John the Baptist stands upon a hill and tradition says that formerly a lighthouse or beacon stood there which was a guide to navigators who travelled over the black waters of the fens in their skiffs and barks. Just below the church hill the land is very flat and was, no doubt, completely covered by water — even now when the river floods this land quickly becomes submerged.

Many of the houses in Holywell were built by Dutch settlers in the 17th century. They came to help drain the land in order to make it suitable for farming. There are still many old houses in Holywell, but the majority of the old houses in Needingworth were destroyed by fire in 1847 and 1855. Two fire-hooks which were used to pull down the burning thatch can still be seen attached to a brick wall in Needingworth High Street, adjacent to Silver Lane. Also in Needingworth, at the top of Overcote Lane, can be seen a lock-up dated 1838 and a memorial to the village inhabitants who lost their lives in the World Wars.

Overcote Lane leads down to The Pike and Eel Inn which stands on the river-side and was originally built in the 16th century. Another very old inn is The Ferry Boat which can be reached by going down to Holywell via Church Street. This is one of the oldest inns in England and is reputed to be haunted!

The village today, especially the Needingworth district, has several new housing estates although there are still a number of listed buildings around.

A church festival is held each June when all the organisations participate in the decoration of the church with flowers, portraying one specified theme. One of the main attractions of the festival is the well-dressing which is beautifully executed by members of the Horticultural Society.

Houghton & Wyton

Houghton and Wyton, adjoining picturesque villages, are situated midway between St Ives and Huntingdon on the north bank of the winding Great Ouse river. Famed for their natural rural beauty the villages offer an interesting mix of thatched and whitewashed cottages, imposing Georgian and Victorian residences redolent with history and ghosts, sturdy dwellings once owned by yeoman farmers and modern brick built houses and bungalows, in all about 600 homes.

The most well known landmark is the timber and brick built watermill which is now a National Trust property visited by many people every year. A mill has stood by the river for over a thousand years.

Cows still wend their way along the village street to their milking parlour passing the oldest house in the villages. Built in the 15th century it was once a public house called the George and Dragon. It faces the green in the centre of Houghton village, which is graced by a thatched clock tower. The marble bust of Potto Brown, the noted local philanthropist gazes sternly over the green. He built the chapel and a school and ran the watermill during the 19th century.

The villages can each boast a church although one is now sadly redundant, two flourishing pubs, a garage, post office and four shops.

The typical occupations of the residents have changed with the years. Previously mainly agricultural, many jobs now involve commuting to London or Cambridge. Many service personnel from the Royal Air Force bases at Wyton and Alconbury also find a home in the villages.

During the summer, Houghton Lock is busy with cruisers and narrow boats. Punts and rowing boats can be hired nearby. The river attracts walkers, ornithologists and anglers all year round.

Ickleton

Ickleton, a village with a population of 500, lies on the west bank of the river Cam near the southern border of Cambridgeshire.

The village was mentioned in the Domesday survey and its

history is recorded on an admirable series of hassocks in St Mary Magdalene's church, Ickleton's most important historic building, which has a working peal of eight bells.

The hassocks show the Roman occupation of Ickleton in AD 43 and carry the story through the Saxons to the Conqueror, through battles, plague and religious intolerance to the arson fire of 1979 which destroyed the chancel roof, the organ, and the medieval painted ceiling under the bell tower. But, perhaps as compensation, the cleaning process after the fire revealed a rare 12th century mural of the Last Supper and events leading up to the Crucifixion and a later Doom painting, which attract many art historians to the church.

Sheep were an all important part of village life and a hundred years ago there were two fulling mills where wool was carded and felted, giving employment to many and leaving a memorial in the family name of Carder, extant in the village today. At that time Ickleton was self sufficient having three butchers, two bakers, two dairies, two tailors, three shoemakers, two grocers, a clockmaker and two weavers. A local family ran the blacksmiths' yard which contained not only five forges manned by eight blacksmiths, but also a paint shop, an ironmonger, a wheelwright's shop and sheds on legs for the seasoning of timber and coffin boards.

An undulation in a field in Top Town marks the position of the saw-pit where travelling sawyers worked long hours of hard, skilled labour. After 14 working days they would 'go on the drink' for seven, frequenting the six public houses then open in the village, which were run by the landlords' wives. Women and children always worked in the fields, and to a lesser degree still do, potato picking, gathering in root crops and pulling wild oats from the growing wheat and barley.

But it was not all work for the people of Ickleton. A charter for a weekly market was granted in 1227, and for 600 years an annual fair was held on July 22nd. This was only discontinued in 1875. Down the years there have been ox roastings, harvest homes, bonfire nights and the ever popular May Day celebrations which gave the children a holiday. The girls would gather paigles (cowslips) and daisies for garlands and dance round the Maypole, singing

'The 1st of May is Garland Day,
Please, I bring my Garland.
The 1st and 2nd and 3rd of May
Are Chimney Sweep and Garland Day'

The village school has become the village hall and children attend schools in Duxford, Sawston and Cambridge. Today, tractors have replaced working horses and far less manual labour is required on the farms. Men and women find work outside the village, which sometimes seems entirely deserted during the day, though a few light industries have recently sprung up in the village itself.

The noise of traffic from the M11 motorway has taken over from the sound of hammer on anvil and the bustle of people and farm animals passing to and fro in the streets. The many ancient charities existing since 1558 were 'United' in 1980, still serving the inhabitants in many ways.

Isleham ﹏

Isleham is a very old place of habitation. There is evidence that people have been living here since prehistoric times and Western Europe's largest hoard of bronze artefacts was found here in 1960. Until 1939 there were no paved roads to the west (Soham) or north (Prickwillow and Ely) and reliance was on one poor road in and out and mainly on green highways (droves) or waterways, though a railway came and went in the span of one man's life. As a result the inhabitants were self sufficient, great traders by water, fiercely independent, and possessed of great skills and hidden abilities, which provided their strength and tenacity.

This independent spirit, and support for Oliver Cromwell in the Civil War, led to the departure to America of the Bernard/Peyton family (who had been lords of the manor since medieval times) at the Restoration of Charles II. Only recently a member of the family, Charles Peyton, again became lord of the manor, but he does not live here.

Charming (many listed) buildings include the 9th century priory church of St Margaret, the beautiful 14th century church of St Andrew with 15th century brasses and a hammerbeam 'angel' roof, a Tudor warehouse, many Elizabethan houses, and almshouses, founded by Lady Frances Peyton in 1582 and still run by trustees.

The Independent chapel in Pound Lane, is one of the earliest 'free' chapels in the country, and it was to this chapel that the famous Evangelist the Rev. Spurgeon came as a young man, from Newmarket, to be baptized at Isleham Ferry in the river Lark on 3rd May 1850. Today there are a church and two chapels, all well-supported with active Sunday schools.

Mature trees are plentiful, new ones are planted yearly, and the parish recreation ground is well used for sports and other functions – the cricket team reached the national village champion's finals at Lords in 1975. The football teams do well and have produced at least three county referees and were playing on winter evenings by floodlight at least 20 years ago! There is a good modern village hall, much used.

The 'Fifties Charity' founded in 1477 for the benefit of the poor, in 1848 paid for the salary of the schoolmaster at the first school in the village and still supplies many extras to the Isleham primary school. It also supports educational projects for those under 25, as well as 'dole' vouchers to purchase food at Christmas for all retired villagers, regardless of need – recipients can always give equivalent money to those less fortunate.

Kimbolton

Kimbolton is set in the gently undulating, partly wooded, agricultural countryside of southwest Cambridgeshire, with Bedfordshire and Northamptonshire as close neighbours. This part of the country was originally Huntingdonshire.

The river Kym runs along the north eastern fringe. There is a wide, mostly Georgian, main street, with buildings having interesting shop fronts and brindled roof tiles. At one end of the street is the castle and at the other the church of St Andrew, built in 1219 but with later alterations. Limited archaeological finds in the vicinity of the old airfield to the north suggest there may have been a small Roman settlement here. By Domesday the population was 500, second only in the county to Huntingdon itself. The layout of Kimbolton was probably the result of the market charter granted in 1200 by King John; from this period dates Newtown and the diversions of the main road through the High Street/Market Place, hence the notorious bends on the now busy A45 (with through traffic from the eastern ports to the Midlands and beyond).

Kimbolton centre and the castle grounds have been designated a Conservation Area of outstanding merit.

The main tourist attraction is Kimbolton Castle (where Catherine of Aragon died in 1536) which was the home of the Dukes of Manchester from 1615 until it was sold to Kimbolton School (originally an Elizabethan grammar school) in 1950. It has an 18th century gateway and outer gatehouse by Robert Adam. The staterooms and extensive grounds are open to the public on Spring and Late Summer Bank Holidays and on some Sunday afternoons in July and August.

In the past decade or so two housing estates – Aragon Place and Castle Gardens – have been built, and at Newtown grazing paddocks are giving way to housing estates where some 160 houses are mushrooming.

Kirtling & Upend ✑

Shown in the Cambridgeshire structure plan as an 'area of outstanding beauty', Kirtling, with the adjoining hamlet of Upend, has a long history dating back to Saxon times. After many unsettled years when the Danes raided the area and several famines occurred, Kirtling estate was given by Earl Godwin to Earl Harold, later King of England. Following the Norman conquest, William I gave the manor to his niece Countess Judith. Several generations passed until the estate was eventually purchased by Sir Edward North in about 1530, and remained with his descendants, until in the 1930s it was bought by the 1st Lord Fairhaven.

The Hall was demolished in 1801, only the Elizabethan gatehouse remaining to this day, to which a house was attached in Victorian times.

The church of All Saints is nearby with parts dating from Norman times. It has a fine doorway with a tympanum of Our Lord in Majesty, a unique collection of hatchments and a number of interesting tombs, the most outstanding of which is that erected to Roger 2nd Baron North in a chapel built to contain it. A comprehensive guide and village history booklet is available at the church.

Most of the residential part of the village lies some distance from the church. It is said that the original village which lay east of the church was abandoned after the Black Death and rebuilt further away. During this century many cottages have been demolished, as the only industry, farming, has become mechanised requiring fewer employees, and this now gives the village a scattered appearance. Nevertheless it is a 'live' village with several generations of the older families still living fairly close to each other.

There are a number of listed buildings and numerous thatched cottages which have been pleasingly restored. The small amount of modern development has been thoughtfully undertaken and blends in well with the older property. There is a most attractive village sign depicting a Saxon and his dog, a well maintained village hall, and a school, which although closed for some years is to be converted to small dwellings, but keeping the same 19th century outward appearance.

With a population of approximately 300, the village has three public houses, the Queens Head, the Beehive, and the Red Lion, all thriving. There is a very successful Cricket Club with a superbly kept pitch, a Women's Institute, an Over 60's Club, a Youth Club, and on the first Saturday in September each year a magnificent show of produce and handicrafts.

The village has a post office and shop combined, a garage (repairs only), stud farms equipped with all the most modern facilities for horses, several large farms and some smallholdings. The water piped from Denver Sluice in Norfolk, destined for use in Essex, is brought to the surface in Kirtling and descends many 'steps' until it reaches the river Stour which rises in the vicinity.

Upend is now designated a 'conservation village', and is a beauty spot especially in spring. It boasts one of the very few listed red telephone kiosks! The churchyard is also a delight in spring when carpeted with snowdrops and at its gate is a VR post box set into the wall.

Landbeach ❧

The name Landbeach is derived from medieval times when sheep were brought here from nearby Waterbeach when the pastures there were flooded. It is still a fairly small village with just over 250 dwellings.

It is worth diverting from the Cambridge to Ely road to come to

Landbeach Tithe Barn

Landbeach. If the wishes of the rector, Robert Masters and the villagers had been granted in 1763, this main road would have been built through the village, but the 'powers that be' at that time decided to ignore the village road and repair the highway, which is now the A10. This decision upset the villagers particularly as they were required 'to do statute work thereon for a certain number of days'. Most fortunate though as far as the present day inhabitants are concerned for although heavy traffic is only half a mile away it is hardly audible. The village is quiet and peaceful, a haven for those living here.

The Baptist chapel is on the left going in the direction of Ely. It is a handsome building, erected in 1854. It was frequently visited by the famous preacher Charles Haddon Spurgeon. If the congregation was too large to fit into the chapel, he would stand on a cattle crib and preach in the field opposite.

The High Street curves through the village giving a pleasant scene each time a corner is turned. The road is bordered by a mixture of dwellings, Victorian, medieval and modern which blend in well and present a pleasant variety. Beyond the houses on either side is farmland which produces mostly arable crops. Asparagus grows particularly well here, a delicacy of which the locals take full advantage.

After you have passed the post office look at the first thatched house on the right. In this house two ladies came to live in 1665. They came to Landbeach from London to escape the plague, but they were too late. They unfortunately died of the illness as did the rector and his son, this family being the only one with whom they had contact. Happily the plague did not spread to any other villagers.

The tithe barn has been acquired for the village by the County Council. Its black timbered frame and massive thatch possess an air of permanence and durability even though the countryside around it has changed. It was built over 400 years ago when a canal ran through the village and barge traffic was common, but little remains of that now.

Walk back, turn left and go on into the parish church of All Saints. Matthew Parker, the most famous of Landbeach rectors preached from the pulpit here. He was rector at a time of great upheaval within the Christian Church, the Reformation. He subsequently was given the honour of becoming the Archbishop of Canterbury in the reign of Queen Elizabeth I. The church is well maintained and contains some fine medieval woodwork and stained glass.

What of the present day inhabitants of Landbeach? It is not wholly a 'commuter village'. A good number live and work on the surrounding farms. There are also local tradesmen such as builders, plumbers and freezer specialists based in the village. Landbeach is fortunate to possess two excellent village shops as well as the post office.

Landbeach is very neatly encapsulated in its Village Sign which shows the church, a thatched cottage, the tithe barn and sheep surmounted by the golden mitre of Matthew Parker.

Leverington 🌿

Leverington is situated two miles north west of Wisbech. It has a population of 4000 but this is increasing every day because of the development of several private housing estates. The village has many amenities for its occupants which include one church, two pubs, three general stores, a post office, butcher's shop, hairdresser, and fish shop. There are also several small industries in the village with seven council-owned mini factories, three engineering workshops, three garages and Colemans' bus station. However the main occupation of the village is fruit, flower and agricultural farming.

In the centre of Leverington stands St Leonard's church, parts of which were built in the 13th century, and it was added to in the 14th and 15th centuries. It stands out as a landmark as it has a beautiful tall steeple set into a Norman turret, with four smaller turrets to support it. The church has a large congregation and during the festive season there is standing room only.

The county primary school is opposite the church and has over 100 pupils. On the site where the school stands today, there used to be a town hall, and 100 years ago there were three schools in the village, a Church school and two others. These three schools were run with financial assistance from the Feoffees Charity. This charity still exists today, but its earliest deed is dated the 9th October 1634, and this refers to an earlier deed dated 20th January, 1555. The general practice had been for the lands to be administered by twelve feoffees, and when six died the survivors were to appoint six additional ones. Money today is issued once a year to the old and widowed of the parish and educational grants are given to the school and to students for scholarships.

The village hall is the centre where many organisations meet. The village also has a large sports field where football and cricket are played regularly. A Sports Field Committee supervises its upkeep. The elderly are also catered for in the village by Roman Court, a warden controlled complex.

Leverington Hall was never a manor house. It was built by the Swaine family in the 17th century. It has a long and somewhat colourful history. At one point the family who owned the hall were so numerous that the kitchen copper was used for preparing the family's meals, as the ordinary domestic appliances were woefully inadequate.

The Chapter House which is of Georgian style was originally the rectory, but recent occupiers include an artist and his family and a Buddhist meditation group. A fire on the night of the 10th May 1986 destroyed most of the building and has saddened the hearts of many villagers, who hope to restore The Chapter House to its former glory.

Park House is a beautiful old house but its exact age is not known. The rear has Tudor characteristics with a Georgian facade. It is beautifully preserved and much of it is in its original state. It is surrounded by park land with many magnificent trees still standing. The Lumpkin family were owners for many years and strong rumour says that Oliver Goldsmith wrote *She Stoops to Conquer* whilst staying at Park House.

Linton 🌿

Iron Age people and later the Romans settled here, but it was the Saxons who not only left a burial ground but also, in AD 725 specifically recorded the place as 'the farmstead in the flaxfields' and so gave Linton its name. The blue of flax which doubtless adorned the area over many centuries was last seen at the farm of Little Linton during and after the Second World War when there were renewed demands for its fibres. To the outsider, this south eastern corner of the county, where the East Anglian Heights provide hilly but open countryside, looks predominantly rural, and it was only when the present century was well advanced that agriculture ceased to be the main occupation.

The river Granta encouraged settlement, and by the Middle Ages there was a thriving market town. Its early importance is revealed in the Conservation Area which consists of the long, narrow High Street, once the main road to Colchester but now bypassed, and a number of adjacent lanes. Here you will find low thatched cottages, jettied timber framed buildings, brick facades, the occasional mansard roof and walls in a succession of white and pastel shades, the pinks reminiscent of bygone days when juice from the ubiquitous sloe was used as colouring for exterior plasterwork.

For a walk within the Conservation Area turn off the High Street into Church Lane flanked by characteristic high flint walls, take a look at the impressive jettied timber framed guildhall dating from the early 1500s and turn into the churchyard shaded by ancient yew trees. The parish church of St Mary the Virgin is a flint faced building which still holds vestiges of its Norman past but is outwardly predominantly Perpendicular. The interior was dramatically refurbished just over 100 years ago when galleries, box pews and three decker pulpit were removed to produce the spaciousness of today.

Continue the walk by crossing the footbridge over the river and once in Horn Lane come to the United Reformed church. Dissent was strong in the 1600s and after the Act of Toleration in 1689 dissenters met openly first in a barn and later in a more permanent building which was followed by the present church built in 1818. The graveyard is noteworthy. A broad path leading up to the church is flanked by massive chest tombs under which lie family burial chambers. Together they form a rare and impressive collection, the subject of a Preservation Order.

'Chandlers' in the High Street, thought to date from the 14th century, is probably the oldest domestic building in the village. On one of its outside walls rests a heavy iron firehook with a 20 ft handle, a reminder of the threat from fire in days when the majority of roofs were thatched. It was used to tear down burning thatch and prevent fire spreading, but must have been an unwieldy thing to handle even when supported on a trolley.

Known sometimes as The Pepperpot, the water tower stands atop Rivey Hill, one of the highest points in the county at just under 370 ft. The tower, Gothic in style with its pierced dark brick walls and slate capped roof, was completed in the mid 1930s, bringing to the village its first piped water. At about the same time another wonder, public electricity, came and both services must have revolutionised domestic life. New building increased and in due time new estates sprang up on the flanks of the old nucleus.

On the south west slopes of Rivey Hill lie the vineyards of Chilford Hundred Wine Company which perpetuates the name by which the area was known in feudal times. Vines of hardy German stock produce white wines made and bottled on the premises. Orders have come not only from this country but from France and as far afield as Japan.

Little Thetford 🦡

Little Thetford is a small village two miles from Ely off the A10. It is possible that it dates back to the Bronze Age as a bronze sickle, rings and pottery have been found in the area. Years ago, the monks of Ely used to come to the river and fish for eels, and in the early days of this century there was a windmill beside the river with a floatbridge manned by the wife of the miller.

The oldest building in the village is St George's church of 14th century origin, consisting of a nave, chancel, north porch and south vestry, with beautiful stained glass windows behind the altar.

In the early days the Baptists worshipped in the open air, later using the clubroom of the Wheatsheaf public house for their meetings, until the existing chapel was built in 1867.

At one time, there were five public houses in the village. The

Wheatsheaf later became the present post office and shop, while the Three Horseshoes and April Thatch later became private houses. On the road between Stretham and Ely were two others, one named Quarterway House, the other The Halfway House also now privately owned dwellings. All the public houses were no doubt justified as many people worked on the land, and looked forward to pleasant evenings drinking with their friends.

The village pond, long since gone, was opposite the Three Horseshoes. There were always ducks swimming around, and it was also used by farmers who would walk their horses through it after working on the fields.

The village school was built in 1871 – prior to that pupils were taught in a hired room lent by the Townsend Charity. One elderly resident recalls paying one penny per week for her education. The school was modernised in 1959 and a special service was held in the church to mark the occasion.

Originally thatched houses and cottages were situated in the main street, but the only thatched houses left standing are Horseshoes, April Thatch and the Round House. The latter, formerly a dovecote, was later converted into two dwellings, until some years ago it was restored to the charming and unique house which it is today. Many of the old cottages and houses have been demolished and replaced by modern houses and bungalows, and all the residents take pride in their gardens.

The old manor house, formerly occupied by farming families, became derelict in the 1970s and was replaced by a row of modern houses.

The house opposite the church known as Church Farm has an interesting history. In 1945 it was a two storey building until the thatched roof caught fire and the top storey was burnt out. A previous resident has recalled that for many years an elderly lady – a churchwarden – had resided there, and after her death strange tapping noises were heard on the long landing. She had walked with a stick, so these noises were attributed to her. After the fire in the house, no more tapping was heard.

Little Wilbraham

Little Wilbraham is a small village, probably best described as a hamlet, which is situated about seven miles from Cambridge, six miles from Newmarket and one mile from its big sister village, Great Wilbraham.

The origins of the village go back to Saxon times, but hardly any evidence of antiquity now remains except for the 12th century church and one or two timber framed Tudor houses and a windmill now, alas, no longer working, but re-designed as an interesting home.

There is a small post office, open three days a week, but no shops. Once there was a butcher's shop on part of Manor Farm which was a thriving business until one day the butcher's indelible pencil accidentally fell into the sausage machine resulting in purple sausages. After this business unaccountably declined!

To the west of the village is Wilbraham Fen, an area of rough and boggy land, but of great botanical interest because of a profusion of wild flowers, peculiar to fenland, which includes Purple Loosestrife, Meadow Rue, Tufted Hair Grass, Harebell and Field Scabious.

There is a no through road in the village which now consists of privately owned and council property. There is also The Hole in the Wall, a 15th century public house and restaurant so named because of the hole in the wall of the building where the farm workers used to come to have their flasks and jugs filled.

It is a pleasant country village whose main purpose is to serve as a dormitory for those of its occupants who work in Cambridge, Newmarket, and surrounding farms.

Littleport ✺

Everyone in the fens knows Littleport, they had riots there didn't they? Yes, as far back as the 13th century the people had rioted against the threatened drainage of the fen when they thought that their livelihood was threatened, but the Littleport Riot of 1816 was an entirely different thing. Farm workers and men returning home from the Napoleonic wars faced unemployment and starvation, and parish relief was scarcely enough to keep body and soul together. The callousness of the Parish Officer eventually goaded the men and they rioted from Littleport to Ely before the military were called in to round them up. Twenty four, including one woman, were sentenced to be hanged. Later 19 of them were reprieved and transported to Botany Bay.

There was great local sympathy for the rioters, and both the builder who had supplied the cart to take five of the condemned to the gallows, and the carpenter who made the coffins soon met their deaths in mysterious circumstances. The five hanged rioters were buried in one grave at Ely, and there is a memorial tablet in the tower of St Mary's church to remind people of the riots. It is interesting to note that the Transport and General Workers Union maintained a rest home at Littleport until quite recently; as good a memorial to the five dead men as they could perhaps have wished.

Legend has it that King Canute founded this fishing village on the Ouse and named it Littleport. Until recently it provided dock and warehouse facilities serving barges from Kings Lynn. Now the cargo port has given way to a modern marina to service the river pleasure boat trade.

Littleport lies five miles north of Ely on the A10, and is set to expand since the by-pass diverted the heavy traffic and at the same time cut the travel time from Cambridge. Population has slowly grown over the past century from 4,157 in 1891 to 5,840 in 1986. Village industry is still largely based on agriculture – packing and transporting vegetables grown on the surrounding fens, but the largest employer has a world famous name, Burberry's Clothing. Burberry's own the 'shirt factory' as it is still called, an industry set up by a Mr Thomas Peacock in 1881 to provide work for the village women during the agricultural depression. He called his company Hope Brothers, wanting to give the villagers something to hope for, and in less than 10 years it was employing 400 workers.

At the turn of the century Littleport was the mecca of ice skating. The moors, close by the railway station, were flooded in winter to provide the finest skating facilities in England. Excursions were run from Liverpool Street, and amid music and bright lighting the skaters raced for prizes ranging from a pig for the local ladies to the Grand Silver Challenge Cup worth 50 guineas and competed for by the world's greatest speed men.

Today, Littleport's big summer attraction is 'the show'. The largest in the Isle of Ely area, it is The East Cambridgeshire Show in all but name. The show is the successor of the old Littleport Feast which took place over three days every July, culminating in a water sports when it is said there was *always* a thunderstorm! The sports traditionally ended with a water polo match and then diving from the top of Sandhill Bridge, but the show is firmly land-based these days!

110

Lode with Longmeadow 🦢

Off the busy B1102, and almost halfway between Cambridge and Newmarket is the village of Lode and its hamlet of Longmeadow. Lode has two unusual features: firstly the road through the village goes nowhere but fades away into the fenland, and secondly it did not receive its own identity until 1894 when a Local Government Board issued an order separating it from Bottisham, and it was formed into a civil parish.

Nevertheless, Lode has existed since the early 13th century, the name meaning a watercourse, the same waterway, probably of Roman origin, on which boats brought up goods to the port of Lode from the Cam, from where they were transported overland to Bottisham.

There existed also the Priory of Anglesey, founded in the reign of Henry I, for canons of the Augustinian Order, and at the time of the Dissolution of the Monasteries some 11 canons were in residence. The property fell into disrepair and passed into many hands including those of Thomas Hobson (1544–1631) the carrier who refused to allow any horse to be taken from his stables in Cambridge except in its proper turn, giving birth to the saying 'Hobson's Choice'; and Sir George Downing, the founder of Downing College in Cambridge. In 1861 the Rev. John Hailstone acquired the property. Hailstone, formerly the vicar of Bottisham, did much good work in Lode. He was responsible for Lode having its own church (1853) and for the building of a school (1865).

In 1926 the Abbey was bought by the first Lord Fairhaven who transformed it into the splendid showpiece that it is today, now administered by The National Trust.

With an area of some 2500 acres, consisting mainly of good farming land, it is no wonder that the main employer has been the land, certainly before the First World War, and for a few years after, either as landworkers or smallholders. The chief crops were oats, barley, wheat, potatoes and during the Second World War and after, sugar beet became a popular crop. A familiar sight of a field of sugar beet being 'singled' or 'chopped out' by an army of workers still remains in the minds of villagers. A small cement works flourished for a time. In these days occupations of the villagers are as myriad as the imagination allows!

A strange character was William Pugh, who became vicar of Bottisham in 1811. Although he was not a Lode man, the people

111

of Lode and Longmeadow benefit from his generosity from the proceeds of a charity that bears his name. He was a man of eccentric ways and of slovenly dress. As a Fellow of Trinity College he caused some concern by keeping to his rooms for days on end and it was said that he wore his linen until the smell became unbearable! He would then wrap it up in newspaper, carry it to the river Cam and drop it in from Trinity Bridge.

Sport is an integral part of village life and the tussle between Lode and Bottisham on the cricket field has over the years been well documented. Reports of the matches during the Victorian era recount the strong rivalry that has always existed between the two villages on the sports field.

Longstanton

Longstanton, seven miles north west of Cambridge, was mentioned in the Domesday Book. Its old name meant 'long stone settlement'. Now three miles long, it was originally two separate villages, All Saints' and St Michael's. The church of All Saints is in use, but St Michael's has become redundant.

The village's most famous family were the Hattons. Sir Thomas Hatton was the cousin of Sir Christopher, Chancellor to Queen Elizabeth I. Hattons lived here in a manor house now gone, until the line died out in 1812. However, the family left their mark – All Saints' church holds all the family tombs and memorials, including a fine chest tomb of the 17th century, with the recumbent figures of Sir Thomas and his wife Mary with their six children. The family crest includes a golden hind, and this emblem caused Sir Francis Drake to rename his ship to honour Sir Christopher, his patron. Longstanton Women's Institute used the Golden Hind emblem on the village sign which they planned and funded in 1982.

Longstanton still retains some interesting old houses and cottages, including some with thatch, and St Michael's area still has some small meadows, old barns and an ancient pond. All Saints' church crossroads is a pretty rural area, with plenty of mature trees. There are still two pumps, one in the High Street built on a platform to allow the carters access and a small domestic pump in Mills Lane. We have lost our windmills, but

Pumb, High St.

The High Street pump, Longstanton

have retained a set of millstones, cleverly used as a paved entrance to St Michael's churchyard.

St Michael's church, churchyard and surrounding area are perhaps the most interesting part of the village. This small attractive church is thatched, one of only two in Cambridgeshire, and it stands in a neat churchyard with a large chestnut tree just inside its gate. Under the tree there is a canopied well with steps leading down to the water. This was a holy baptism well, thought to be very old. In 1986 the villagers restored it and replaced its railings.

The village contains a mixture of housing – three groups of Army houses, because this is home to Oakington Barracks (which is in Longstanton, not Oakington!), an area of council housing which includes attractive bungalows for the elderly, with resident warden, and new houses and bungalows, privately owned, set out in pleasant closes or built behind existing hedges or tree cover, and blended in with the old. One road has a nicely landscaped pond and resident ducks.

The village is surrounded by agricultural land growing wheat, oil seed rape, corn on the cob etc and there are numerous smallholdings. There are still a few farms with a little livestock. The area was once known for its fruit growing but the closure of the railway line meant that growers no longer had a convenient way to send their produce to market. Many smallholders put out roadside stalls selling vegetables, fruit and flowers.

There have been Longstanton witches in the past. The most famous story concerns a Quaker woman, accused by a young woman, Mary Pryor, of having turned her into a bay mare and ridden her all the way to Madingley Hall! Fortunately for the Quaker woman, Mary's story was not believed by the judge at the trial. Even in Victorian times there was a well known local witch with strange powers.

Longthorpe 🪸

Longthorpe is a small but recently expanded village situated about two miles west of the centre of Peterborough. The village dates back to Roman times when it had a strong Roman garrison with a large fortress housing the vast legions and auxiliaries on the site where Thorpe Wood golf course is now situated.

The Tower was commissioned by William de Thorpe as a folly

and is situated almost at the centre of the present village. It has six ft thick walls and was originally three storeys high. One of the interesting features of the Tower is the wall paintings on the interior which were only discovered after the Second World War. They are quite unique and depict the seven ages of man, the five senses, kings and queens and many birds and animals common to the fens of which, of course, Peterborough is at the heart.

St Botolph's Church, thought to be Saxon, was originally a chapel of ease, and its original site was at the junction of West-wood Park Road and Thorpe Road, and was known as either Longthorpe chapel or the chapel of ease. It was rebuilt at Long-thorpe on its present site in 1263. The church itself boasts a magnificent bishop's chair and has an interesting leper's window.

Thorpe Hall was built between 1653 and 1656 and was com-missioned for the Lord Chief Justice Oliver St John. It passed to Lord Fitzwilliam in 1793. (Originally much of Longthorpe and the surrounding area belonged to, or formed part of, the Fitzwilliam estate). After Thorpe Hall ceased to be a family residence it was unused for many years and the last long term use was that of a convalescent home run by the local health authority. There are currently plans for its use as a Sue Ryder Hospice.

The Hall originally boasted a beautiful panelled library but this was removed some years ago and is now restored in its original form in Leeds Castle, Kent.

Holywell at Longthorpe was the termination of the track known as Abbots Walk which led from the Abbey (prior to the present cathedral).

In the present day Longthorpe is proud of its executive housing whilst retaining old world charm and character with its thatched post office and cottages. The past few years have seen the admini-stration offices of Pearl Assurance, Thomas Cook and the regional headquarters of the Trustee Savings Bank moving to the outskirts of the village.

Madingley 🌿

Madingley is an attractive village set amidst farm and woodland about four miles from Cambridge. There is a population of approximately 180 people. The village boasts an Elizabethan hall which was begun in the early 16th century by John Hynde, who died in 1550. His son, Sir Francis Hynde, completed the building, but in order to achieve this he pulled down and used some of the materials from St Etheldreda's church at Histon. The oak hammer beam can be seen in the roof structures of the hall. It is said that the ghost at Madingley Hall is the distressed Lady Ursula Hynde, mother of Sir Francis.

In 1948 the University of Cambridge bought the land and dwellings (then some 1200 acres). The hall itself is now used by the Board of Extra Mural Studies, being self sufficient with lecture and residential facilities.

The present church of Mary Magdalene, dates from the 12th century. It has a 13th century nave and 15th century porch. The Norman font to be seen in the church was brought from St Etheldreda's church at Histon; also to be seen is a 600 year old bell (disused) and memorials to the Cotton family.

The school (1844) remains operational despite a setback. When the well loved teacher Mrs Gwen Ruddle MBE retired after some 39 years in 1978, the village fought but lost the battle against the Local Education Authority's intention to cease to maintain or provide education in the parish. However, residents never gave up their commitment and the project made national and international headlines when they were assisted by an un-named person in their purchase of the building from the Church of England. Now the school is a successful parents' co-operative project – even though the struggle to raise funds is ever present.

The original windmill at Madingley was blown down in July 1909. The mill still standing (though now without sails) was brought from Ellington, Huntingdonshire as a replacement and was re-erected by Mr C. Ison of Histon in 1928. This project was paid for by Mr Ambrose Harding of Madingley Hall.

The Co-op grocery, the baker or the butcher's vans have not been seen delivering in the village for well over a decade; and the typically small village post office closed its doors in 1987. Alas too, the blacksmith's shop was pulled down together with five cottages in the mid 1970s to make way for new bungalows in High Street. Other changes in the village have brought about the loss of four farms (Middle Farm, New Farm, Highfields, and High Arden). The surviving two are Burnt Farm and Home Farm. The housing development at Granary Court was partly created from some old barns on Home Farm. Beck Brook Farm came onto the scene in the early 1980s.

International history is reflected in Madingley by way of the Cambridge American Cemetery and Memorial depicting the conflicts of the Second World War. The 30.5 acres of land, donated by the University of Cambridge, is situated on a gentle slope overlooking the East Anglian countryside towards Ely Cathedral.

Maxey 🦡

Maxey village has a heritage steeped in history. Many of its quaint stone buildings were built hundreds of years ago. The village post office building dates back to the 17th century.

The powerful sounds of a working watermill can be heard at Maxey. An 18th century building, it dates back to 1779. The age-old process of grinding corn has not been changed. In times past household flour used to be milled here. The present owner, Mr Staples, has restored it to its present glory.

There is a very important historical site. A team of archaeologists have discovered that the area contains relics of the Neolithic age including the only polished-stone axe to be excavated in England this century.

The parish church of St Peter was built in about 1113 AD, in order to serve the needs of three hamlets: Maxey, Lolham and Nunton. Maxey the largest of the three has grown, whilst the others have dwindled. The Lady chapel was built in 1367. On the south wall of the chapel is a wooden plaque recording Mary Walsham's legacy. She died in 1745 and left £100, the interest from which was to be distributed to the poor of the parish in bread or money, as the minister and churchwardens thought desirable.

The altar is an oak table and scribbled underneath in pencil is 'John Francis Hardy made the table in December 1826'. The church has six fine sounding bells.

The present day Castle Farm was once 'Maxey Castle'. Margaret Beaufort, mother of Henry VII resided here, presiding over the Deepings as lady of the manor in the year 1458.

In recent years one of the major changes in the village was the closing of the Maxey primary school and the transfer of pupils to the nearby village school at Northborough. The school was bought by the villagers and is now used as Maxey Community Centre.

The village is practically surrounded by water. These old gravel workings have been well landscaped, giving some very pleasant waterside walks.

Melbourn ✍

Melbourn is situated either side of the A10 between Royston and Cambridge. It has about 1,600 houses.

It has been suggested that Melbourn meant 'Melda's river'. Melda lived in Anglo Saxon days at the Bury. It was the largest and most important house in the village. On the site springs a stream, which in 1086 ran nine mills, none of which are left today.

In 1690 William Ayloffe provided a free school for the children of Melbourn. This was held above the south porch of the church. Much later, in 1818, John Trigg left a large sum of money in his will for Melbourn children's education. This helped to found the primary school which is still in use today.

All Saints church standing at the cross is of Norman origin. It was badly damaged during the Reformation and was subsequently repaired and rebuilt where necessary. One panel on the font still shows Norman arcading work.

The United Reformed church in Orchard Road was originally the Meeting House built in 1720. It is one of the oldest of its type in the country.

Lordship Farm, once known as Argentine Manor, was mentioned in the Domesday Book. Parts of the existing house in the High Street are 800 years old and there is still a Norman well in the cellar.

Further along the High Street are 'Sheeps Head Row' cottages. They were named this by a coach driver, who said that every time he drove through Melbourn with the mail, a head would appear from the upper window of each cottage. They looked, he said, like a row of sheep's heads hanging outside a butcher's shop!

There is a rare fire engine house in Station Road, built in 1847. This has been renovated on the instructions of the Parish Council and the original wording on the doors reinstated.

Melbourn today is a thriving community. It has a village college that serves 13 villages. Its buildings are used for a variety of activities. Melbourn has only three pubs now, but at one time, when the village was approximately half of its present size it sported 20 pubs! It has all the shops necessary for its day-to-day needs. The industrial estate to the south of the village is now well established and the newer science park towards the north end is rapidly filling up with both established and new companies.

Meldreth 🦢

The village of Meldreth lies nine miles south west of Cambridge. The river Mel, a tributary of the Rhee later to become the Cam, runs through the village. In the past Meldreth was a thriving fruit growing area and special mention must be made of the Meldreth greengage, renowned for its flavour. Today arable farming has taken over from the orchards.

Holy Trinity church has stood, on the same site as an earlier wooden one, for almost 500 years. In the tower there are eight bells, the earliest dated 1617 and the newest 1968. Companologists from all over the world visit this famous peal.

At one time there were several manors and watermills, of these Topcliffe's Mill still remains. In recent years it has been partially restored. There were few large houses and most of the population lived in small thatched cottages made of lath, plaster and clunch. Today's residents mostly live in modern houses with a sprinkling of old world properties. Workers commute to Cambridge, London and other distant places although a few work in the village where there is one large factory and several smaller enterprises.

Village celebrities include Andrew Marvell, the 17th century poet, who lived at the Court and wrote some of his poems there in the oak room. The niece of Neville Chamberlain lived at the Gables and in the same house many years before a young son murdered his mother.

Under a large chestnut tree on Marvell's Green stand the stocks and whipping post last used in the 1860s. Beside them can be seen the stone base of an ancient praying cross. Meldreth Manor (the Manor of Stretes) was given by the owners in the early 1960s to the Spastics Society who built in the grounds a residential school for 120 multi-handicapped children.

The population today is approximately 1700 and well served by several shops, post office, primary school, village hall and public transport. In Victorian days there were six public houses but today only one remains. One of these pubs, near the church, belonged to a local brewery (Jarmans) and this house may well have been the guildhall as it still contains a dragon beam. Although this attractive village with a long history has seen many changes in recent years it still retains a rural atmosphere and a strong community spirit.

Mepal ✤

Mepal today is a small agricultural fenland village lying about half a mile off the Fen Trunk Road between Chatteris and Ely. Ireton's Way leads north to Chatteris, built to improve communications by Oliver Cromwell's engineers under General Ireton, straight as an ancient Roman road, over the Old and New Bedford Rivers.

The rivers were part of Vermuyden's fen drainage system – the Old Bedford being cut before the Civil War and the New Bedford, or Hundred Foot Drain, after it. The washes, which lie between the two, act as grazing fields in the summer and, becoming inundated by flood water in winter, are a natural refuge for wildfowl. The Gault Hole from which clay used to be dug for brickmaking, lies to the west of the village. The hole, now marshy, is a nesting place for swans and herons can be seen there occasionally.

The fens to the north of the village used to be frozen over for 4–8 weeks annually and local competition was fierce in the Ice Skating Championships, speed not style being essential!

South of the village lies the area known as Mepal Airfield. Now farmland, the 75th RNZAF Squadron flew Stirlings and Lancasters operationally during the Second World War and still retain affectionate links with local people. After the war the airfield briefly served as a Thor missile base.

One of Vermuyden's adventurers, James Fortrey, built Fortrey Hall, 'a commodious habitation', on the riverside, to which he retired when James II was exiled. The hall had its own bridge over the Old Bedford River, and was said to be just a day's walk away from Ely Cathedral for the monks on pilgrimage from Ramsey and Thorney.

Mepal is not mentioned in the Domesday Book, but St Mary's church, which has neither steeple nor tower, can be dated to the 12th century, and there are mentions of 'Mephale' in the Ely Diocese records from 1132.

One hundred years ago there were five public houses and a brewery in the village, today only one remains – The Three Pickerels. Near this pub is a farm, one of whose outbuildings has the date 1765 built into the brickwork. This was one of the sheds surrounding the old Market Place, which was later known as Cluncher's Yard when clunch, or soft sandstone, was quarried from the river bank and stored there before being ferried away by barge.

The village school was built in 1874 to accommodate some 80 children of varying ages. Attendance would seem to have been erratic depending on agricultural requirements for 'hands' and, during bad weather, the passage of the ferry boat across the marshes. A modern school was built in 1966 some 100 yards away in Brangehill. The old building with its lovely windows and inherent memories of children's coats drying by the fire has been acquired as the village hall.

Opposite is a small village green where the local WI have erected a village sign depicting Vermuyden's wooden bridge with grazing sheep. The other, larger village green is the scene of the continuing annual Mepal Feast in September.

Mereside

Mereside is now technically a hamlet, as it has neither church nor school. The old Baptist Chapel has recently been renovated into two private homes, and the local children are 'bussed' to school.

Set in agricultural country, this area is rich fenland, with few trees but many waterways. Sugar-beet, potatoes and wheat are the main crops, though at onion time the aroma from the fields is quite savoury.

Once, all the inhabitants either worked on the large farms or rented County Council smallholdings, now the majority travel to the towns for work.

The through road with houses on either side, which once hummed only with tractors and associated farm vehicles, now has to contend with commuter cars hurrying to work, and container lorries, servicing the rapidly increasing population's needs.

Milton 🌿

In the 1920s Milton was an interesting community of about 500 adults and children. It had its own school which bore the date 1836, the children being divided into three classes of about 30 children in each class.

Work was plentiful as there were several farms and, at busy times of the year, the workers helped out on each other's farms to get the crops planted or harvested. Gravel was dug and large gravel pits formed. Another company manufactured roof tiles. There were nurseries, one specializing in tomatoes and cucumbers, the other one selling bedding plants, general garden plants and seeds which were sent all over the country as a result of orders from their catalogue. A flourishing laundry business was carried on by the Goodin family and this is still owned by the same family today.

Milton had its share of characters. For example, when speaking to older residents and the name Vashti Wilkin is mentioned, many will claim with pride that she brought them into the world. It would seem she was a tower of strength to the wives and the first to be sent for on the occasion of a birth. Time meant nothing to her as she would turn out whatever the hour and be prepared to stay however long the labour. It is said she was also there at life's end, helping with the laying out of the dead and the comfort of the bereaved. These services were given and no payment was expected by her.

A community, such as Milton, required a blacksmith as horses were used on the land. Mr Butcher filled this position having his forge in the centre of the village near the pond and water pump. He must have been a stalwart of the church as he was a verger, stoked the boilers, rang the bells, wound the church clock and blew the organ bellows, whilst his wife kept the church clean!

The second Sunday in May was Feast Sunday, being quite a highlight of the year for the residents as Thurston's Amusements arrived, bringing the Gallopers or Sedgewick's Ark, together with sideshows of quoits, darts and coconut shies. A set of swinging boats was an essential part of the show.

In times past, Milton had several thatched cottages, but now only two of the houses leading to the church are thatched. The church has quaint gargoyles on its 13th century tower. Through-

Baits Bite Lock, Milton

out its history the church has featured prominently in village life and, today, there has been much effort and thought to form a Children's Hospice in the house which was the old rectory.

Milton today is very different from the 1920s as high-technology science is encouraged on the new Milton Science Park. The village was earmarked a few years ago for a 5,000 house development with all the accompanying shopping facilities. Some of the houses are already built and occupied – but, to date, the village maintains a lively community spirit with many social activities centred around the church and community centre.

Regrettably, the appearance of the old village has almost gone, leaving only a few houses, the river, and pretty Baitsbite Lock to remind us of the past.

Murrow 🦑

The original settlement of Murrow dates back to Roman times and existed on high land where a road was built along a bank. This was long before the draining of the fens.

Today's village covers an area of about four square miles, although not densely populated and more homes are being built all the time, with surrounding land down to arable farming.

In the first half of this century, the village was inhabited almost entirely by railway and land workers. But the railway, once famous for its one of only two 'diamond crossings', where the Midland and Great Northern crossed the London and North Eastern, is now closed. There were two stations and daily, fresh produce, fruit, vegetables and grain were brought to the station in horse drawn wagons, to be taken by rail to markets all over the country.

With modern machinery, fewer men are needed for working the land, and so there is less casual work for the women, strawberry picking and spring flowers being the only things locally needing such labour. They even have machines for hoeing sugar beet seedlings! Therefore more and more people travel by car to nearby towns and cities, to work in offices, shops and factories.

There is a Methodist chapel and a church, but regular congregations are small, though the villagers would be loathe to see either close. The church is unique in that the altar is at its north end. It was built in 1857 as a chapel of ease, and is called Corpus Christi. The vicar is shared by two adjoining villages, a common sign of modern times.

At one time there were a total of five public houses, but this has dwindled down to one now, The Bell.

In 1978 a tract of land was acquired by the villagers to lay a playing field. To pay for the general upkeep of the field, a Gala Week is held annually in July with functions for the entire population to participate in.

Newborough & Borough Fen 🦑

The parish of Newborough is very new, having been formed in 1823. The church, dedicated to St Bartholomew, was erected in

1830. The Church of England school dates back to 1852. The money came from the proceeds realised from the sale of part of Borough Fen estate at the time of the enclosures in 1822. Around the church are the oldest houses. The school, of course, has been extended with all modern improvements. At the turn of the century a few new houses were built, and after the First World War some council homes were added. After the Second World War, a large council estate was built, then private estates started springing up, so that the village has grown considerably.

Newborough is a very large and scattered parish, and includes a hamlet called Milking Nook, approximately a mile away from the village. This is easily as old as the main village and got its name because in the 18th and 19th centuries farmers from neighbouring villages grazed their animals there. Each village had their own droves, i.e. Barnack, Northborough, Bainton and Glinton. These roads still exist today, but bear no relevance to their situation.

Agriculture really is the only local industry and the area is made up of a few large farms, but is also dotted with smaller ones, where enterprising families have struggled to get a living.

On the southern and south western boundary runs the ancient Roman Car Dyke, which is unspoilt and a haven for wildlife.

Borough Fen consists of around 3000 acres, and was originally waste and commonland belonging to the Abbey of Peterborough. Then by Act of Parliament 1812, land was allotted to the common land tenants, but some was sold for drainage expenses. This was the first drainage to take place. The inhabitants at this time occupied a few farmhouses and scattered cottages. In 1920, however, the Soke of Peterborough County Council bought most of the land for smallholdings, chiefly for ex-servicemen.

The gem of Borough Fen is the Duck Decoy. The earliest reference is in 1670, when the Decoyman (Mr Williams) was granted permission to pierce the river Welland to lead water to his decoy pond. The Decoy was continuously managed by the Williams family until the death of Billy Williams in 1958, who was well known in the district. In 1951 the Wildfowl Trust undertook the financial responsibility of ringing the ducks that are caught, instead of killing them and the decoy is the oldest of the few decoys surviving.

Newnham 🎍

Until the middle of the last century, Newnham had very few buildings, most of which were in Newnham Road and around the mill. It was not until the end of the 19th century that further building began and Newnham grew as we know it today. Towards the latter part of the 13th century, a Carmelite friary existed somewhere near the mill, which seems to have been a focal point for centuries. The mill race was supposed to have been cut before the Domesday Book to serve the mill. The mill as we see it now, was rebuilt after a fire in 1853. In 1977 it was refurbished without losing its character, now being the restaurant known as 'Sweeney Todd'.

When in 1882 the Fellows of the colleges at Cambridge were allowed to marry, a lot of big houses were built for them and their families, and smaller houses were built for the college servants and employees. The infant school, first mentioned in 1874, was situated where the petrol station is now sited. Newnham Croft School, as it is now known, was moved to its present position in 1925.

Next to the petrol station are the Perse Almshouses, re-erected in 1886. In the will of Stephen Perse, MD, Fellow of Gonville & Caius, who died in 1625, money was left for 'Six several low tenements of one room apiece to be built near his free school, for six several Almsfolk, poor, aged and unmarried women, to be at least over 40 years and parishioners of St Edward's, St Michael's or St Benet's. The appointments to be made by the Master of Caius and some fellows ... each inhabitant to receive £26 per annum.'

The Malting House, one of Newnham's landmarks, was rebuilt in its present form a few years before the First World War. The original building is believed to have been built 100 years beforehand. The very narrow Maltings Lane leads right to Ridley Hall, the theological college, and left to Church Rate Walk. With its old cottages and narrow lane it is completely unspoiled and beautiful.

The first church in Newnham was a wooden building which stood between the present church and vicarage. It was a mission church in the parish of Grantchester. In 1885 the parish room, now a flourishing community centre, with two rooms above it, was built: and in 1889 the vicarage for the curate was completed. The foundation stone for the present church was laid in 1900, and on St Mark's day in 1901 the church was dedicated by the Bishop of Ely. But it was not until 1918 that St Mark's became a separate parish.

As for the present? A lot of infilling has taken place of course, but on the whole, looking at old photographs, Newnham Croft has changed little. Cows and horses are still grazing on Sheeps Green, which in the spring looks like a yellow carpet when covered with buttercups. There are still many old trees and those that were destroyed by storms have been replaced by new ones.

Newton

Newton is a delightful, small village in South Cambridgeshire. It has a long recorded history having been first mentioned in a document of AD 975 and there is evidence of even earlier, Romano-British, occupation of the area.

In medieval times most of the land was owned by the monks of Ely. Newton was one of 33 Ely manors and Newton people had to produce a quota of food for the monks as well as meeting other feudal obligations. The manor court ruled the village and there was a manor farmhouse here.

After the Dissolution of the Monasteries the manor passed to the Dean and Chapter of Ely Cathedral. They leased the manor to local men like the farmer John Swan in the 16th century and to others, such as Dr John Hills, a Canon of Ely and Dr Gideon Harvey of Middlesex, a physician, during the 17th century. Later, the manor lease passed to the Hurrell family, a member of which was able to buy the reversion of the lease in the mid 19th century. The estate remains with a member of the Hurrell family to this day.

Agriculture remained almost the only source of employment for the men of the village well into the 20th century. Only domestic work and seasonal field work was available to women.

By the second half of the 19th century there were two substantial houses in Newton. One, Newton Hall, was built in the 1850s by a local landowning family, the Pembertons. The other was the home of the Hurrell family. At about the time of the purchase of the freehold of the estate, the purchaser, William Hurrell, demolished the old manor farmhouse and, in its place, built a new house in the Victorian–Tudor style and called it The Manor.

The Hurrell family had a good reputation for concern for the welfare of village people and, by the 1890s, had established evening classes in basic subjects. At about this time a bachelor son of the family, Harold Hurrell, became very interested in the Arts and Crafts movement of the time. He established a Metalwork Evening School in Newton which flourished for several decades. An official report of the time gives a good indication of its standing and importance. Austin Keen, Education Secretary for Cambridgeshire County Council wrote in 1902:

'The grandest work in this direction that I know of is done by Mr Hurrell of Newton. Last year the Newton school turned out £219 worth of metalwork, producing a substantial profit for the workers. This occupies six months of the year. As soon as the spring is fairly in, the school is closed and the men are encouraged to work on the gardens and allotments. Nor is the school simply a manufacturing or producing one; the educational side of the work is by no means neglected. The young men are systematically taught drawing and designing especially as applied to their repousse work, forging, soldering, metal plating and enamelling. It is intensely interesting to see a group of agricultural labourers collectively working out the details of an elaborate design in which probably each of the branches above-mentioned is illustrated and applied – all of them exercising an intelligent knowledge of the detailed drawings and a splendid enthusiasm in translating them into metal form. For such men life has an additional significance to anything the day school ever imparted.'

As early as the mid 1890s work was being exhibited in London and the prestigious *Studio* magazine reported on and named Newton work and craftsmen.

In many households in Newton, especially in those of older people, there are treasured articles of worked copper which were made by their friends and relatives in the Metalwork School. It continued to function until the 1940s. As a result of the regular London exhibitions Newton work was widely known and orders were executed for people all over the country. The work included inn signs, ecclesiastical objects, lamps, vases, war memorials and much else. A copper lamp, made in the school, was put up at the cross-roads as a memorial to Harold Hurrell after his death in the 1920s.

Although Newton remains a small village it continues to have agreeable links with a wider area as it had in the days of the Metalwork School. Every year talented local residents write and produce a pantomime, which runs to five performances and is seen by many people who come from beyond the village. Every day visitors from afar visit the village pub, the Queens Head, a former coaching inn, on the old turnpike road from Cambridge to Ware. It has become famous nationally through the Egon Ronay Guides.

Local people have a justifiable sense of pride in Newton.

Newton in the Isle 🌿

Situated in the north of the county this Newton is a small village just in Cambridgeshire, but on the borders of Lincolnshire and Norfolk.

Passing through on the B1165, about four miles from Wisbech, on the main road through the village you will see the village sign.

The figure on the sign is of Sir John Colvile, the most famous of the Colviles, who were the lords of the manor of Newton since the time of the Norman Conquest. Sir John fought at the Battle of Agincourt with King Henry V. He founded the college or chantry called the Chapel of St Mary in the Marsh or 'Capella Maris' in 1403 and endowed it with £40 per annum to maintain four chaplains, four clerks and ten poor men. The college depicted on the sign stood on the old Roman bank near to the old rectory. Strange to think the sea came so close.

The white lion rampant has been part of the Colvile coat of arms since 1280. The six bells denote the six bells on St James' parish church, built in the 13th century. On the right hand side of the sign there is a woad plant. Woad was grown to the end of the last century in Newton and probably pressed in the woad mill at Parson Drove. In the present day, one local pub is called The Woadman's Arms and the other The White Lion. The latter has the lion rampant as its sign.

The original Hall in Newton had a series of sitting rooms opening into each other to form a gallery. Over the mantelpiece in the servants' hall was a sign which said 'Whosoever sits down and says not Grace, sits down a fool and gets up an ass'. Only the cellars remain under the present Hall – rebuilt in 1807.

The first school was built on glebe land in 1853 and financed by the church. By 1928 it was forced to give up the struggle against inflation and poor conditions. The County Council took over and built a new school, opened in 1930 and called The Colvile School.

The new school existed for 57 happy years but because of the falling birthrate and financial cutbacks, sadly the school has closed and the name of Colvile faded out, though there is still a Colvile Road in the village.

Northborough 🍃

The village of Northborough is situated on the A15, seven miles north of Peterborough. Northborough was first mentioned in the 12th century Survey of Northamptonshire, although there is evidence of an earlier settlement.

Originally, the village was built round the church and manor house, this being the oldest part of the present village and boasts many fine stone and thatched cottages. There are no further plans for expansion in the village.

The manor house, or Northborough Castle as it is known today, is believed to have been built by the de la Mare family around the mid 14th century. The manor was bought in 1563 by James Claypole and it is through this family that the village was to become connected with Oliver Cromwell due to the marriage of his daughter, Elizabeth to John Claypole. Since these early times, the manor has been owned by several families and at present is privately owned.

The parish church of St Andrew has been described as 'a monument of disappointed hopes and unaccomplished ambitions', giving the impression of being 'more curious than beautiful'. This is due to the mixture of architectural styles from the 12th to 14th centuries, each period of building being incomplete, probably due to lack of funds. An interesting part of the church is its Norman bell-cote which is one of three within the local area. There are only two bells, one dated between 1359 to 1380 and the other dated 1611. Once again the village link to Oliver Cromwell is apparent as his wife was buried here on 19th November 1665. St Andrew's also provides a resting place for Martha, widow of John Clare the poet (who lived in the village for 10 years). As well as the parish church the village also has a Methodist chapel which was built in 1869.

Over the years there have been several public houses and drinking places, two of the better known being the Cuckoo Inn which is now sadly only remembered as a bus stop and the

Northborough village

Packhorse which is the only existing public house. The Cuckoo
Inn and the Packhorse were village shops as well.

The original school was built around 1877 and can still be seen
situated on the A15 opposite the manor, this is now a private
dwelling. The new school was built in 1966 to accommodate the
growth in population and the merger of Maxey and Northborough schools in 1969.

To show that Northborough once was a village with influence,
during the late 13th century an annual fayre was held on the 14th
August. This fayre was surrendered by Geoffrey de la Mare, lord
of the manor, due to injury it caused to the Abbot of Peterborough's fayre. Nowadays this has been replaced by an annual
family day. In the days the village could boast a pond, ice skating
matches used to be held, but now the only local village ice skating
is held at Baston Fen, Lincs, approximately five miles north and
this is obviously dependent upon the weather.

Oakington 🦢

The name Oakington – Hockington in the Domesday Book – has
nothing to do with oak trees but is a corruption of 'Hoca's tun'.
The discovery, in 1928, of three Anglo-Saxon skeletons buried in
shallow graves, one of them with a shield over its shattered skull,
suggests that this was the site of an ancient battlefield. The part
played by more recent warriors, RAF Oakington in the Second

131

World War, is recognised by a bas relief of a bomber flying across a blue sky on the village sign.

The village today is roughly centred on the parish church of St Andrew, 13th century with a 12th century nave. The fabric is in excellent condition, almost all the repair work having been done during the last decade by enthusiastic church members and their families. The church has not, however, always been in such good heart and indeed, in 1683, the Bishop described the parish of Oakington as 'the most evil' and 'most full of vice' in his diocese. Presumably this was because most of the parishioners refused to go to church at all, preferring to listen to itinerant preachers in the great barns of East Anglian farmers. For Oakington lies in the heart of Cromwell country and throughout the 17th century was a stronghold of religious independence.

The most famous of the dissenters was the Congregationalist Francis Holcroft, known as 'The Apostle of East Anglia'. He was buried in 1692 just outside Oakington churchyard by the side of his assistant Joseph Oddy and Henry Osland, the pastor of the first Congregationalist church in the area. For many years visitors to the 'Oakington Graves' have assumed that the dissenters had been denied burial in sanctified ground, but recent research has shown that the non-conformists had bought a field adjoining the church-yard as a cemetery of their own.

At the extreme north east of the parish boundary is the railway line from March to Cambridge. It came to the small village of Oakington in 1846 because the much larger village of Cottenham wanted nothing to do with it. As a result, market gardeners from the fenlands beyond had to bring all their apples, cabbages, strawberries, asparagus and cut flowers to the goods yard at Oakington which also handled great numbers of milk churns and mountains of domestic coal. Sadly the station was closed down in 1970 and today the only trains passing through are gravel trains from pits originally opened up to provide jobs for unemployed farm labourers.

No description of Oakington would be complete without a mention of one of the oldest villagers, the white-bearded 'Snowy' Farr. Snowy, a retired roadman, has devoted his energies to raising money for charity by exhibiting his collection of pet animals with whom he has an uncanny rapport. He can often be seen in the village, immaculate in a scarlet guardsman's tunic, leather gaiters and a silk top hat, riding a flag-bedecked tractor or pedalling an old, gaily painted ice-cream tricycle on his way to the Saturday market at Cambridge or to other charitable events.

The Offords

The Offords are comprised of Offord Cluny and Offord D'Arcy. Offord Cluny has a current population of 440 compared with 170 in 1801. Before the Domesday survey in 1086 Arnulf de Hesding made the gift of an estate in the village to the Abbey of Cluny, a town in Burgundy, France. When the monks left after 300 years the name remained. Offord Darcy has a population of 720 today, compared with 156 in 1801 and owes its name to the Dacy family who held land there in 1220.

Each village has its own church though they were united in one parish in 1976. All Saints in Offord Cluny was built in the 13th

Offord Post Office

century and St Peter's, Offord Darcy was built in 1130. Services are held mainly in All Saints as St Peter's is designated a redundant church. Other features of the villages are Offord Cluny manor house built in 1704 and Darcy manor built in 1607. The old school opened in 1875 and was replaced in 1988 by a new school on the existing site.

The railway was constructed in 1850. The main employers in the village are fruit and vegetable packers and grain merchants. Farming also plays an important part in the life of the community, being mostly arable.

The post office is situated in Offord Cluny with an adjoining general grocery store. Also in Offord Cluny is the petrol station/haulage contractor. Offord Darcy has a general store and a bakery. Each village also has its own public house. The main leisure activities are fishing, boating, canoeing, riding, rambling and the river attracts many visitors to the village during the summer.

Orton Longueville

A village once occupied by the Romans and now grown to accommodate the increasing population of Peterborough, it nevertheless retains its old world charm and history. Orton Longueville is mentioned in the Domesday Book.

Roman remains of the 2nd and 4th centuries were discovered in 1907 and in the 1960s a basilica was found and now lies under a modern housing estate, namely Orton Malborne.

The village street meanders for about 700 metres ending at the southern end at a non-motorised lane, by the name of Moggeswell! Also at this end is a large village green complete with a magnificent chestnut tree but unfortunately, no blacksmith.

The church of the Holy Trinity is c1240. It still retains its sanctus bell and also a bell cast in Plantagenet times. There is a splendid wall painting from the 16th century and a very fine sculpture of Lady Mary Seymour of Chantrey. One must not forget the stone effigy of an armoured knight.

Standing adjacent to the church is Orton Hall built by the then Marquis of Huntly and Aboyne and occupied by that family for many years. It was built of the famous Barnack ragstone from the nearby Barnack quarry, many of the houses in the village and also the church are built of the same stone. The hall was extended in 1855. The avenue leading up to the hall is flanked by magnificent Wellingtonia trees which are of course protected. The hall is now a girls school.

Although Orton Longueville is encircled by modern housing, one can still wander through the village and see interesting buildings of yesteryear.

Orton Waterville 🐚

Orton Waterville lies just off the A605, three miles west of Peterborough and two miles east of the A1.

Orton, an abbreviation of Overton, means 'farm on the slope or hill'. After the Conquest the Waterville family owned the manors of Overton and Thorpe as tenants to the Abbots of Peterborough, and gave their name to the village.

A local historian W. T. Mellows stated in a report given in 1922, 'Overton Waterville is an unspoilt medieval village. The church, the manor house and the ancient homesteads remain. Traces of the open field system may still be recognised in the lands at the back of the town street. Long may it continue as a place of delight to the lover of antiquity, a surviving example of the village of our forefathers.'

Early in the 16th century the manor belonged to the wardens and scholars of the Pembrook College.

In 1801 the population was 270, in 1931 it was 315. However, the proximity of Orton Waterville to Peterborough led to the development of land to the east of the village – Lady Lodge estate. By 1971 the population was 1,300 and in 1985 it was 6,500.

There are a number of interesting houses, some of them thatched. Many Roman relics found here are now in the Peterborough Museum. Manor Farm dates from Elizabethan days and part of the rectory is almost as old. A 15th century dovecote stands in the garden.

The village church retains some Norman work in the nave, but it was largely rebuilt in the Early English period and added to about a century later. One of its doors has been here since the reign of Elizabeth 1, as has the oak pulpit, which is one of the most magnificent of its kind in the country. Richly carved, it rises from a tapered base with panelled sides, above a frieze of foliage, beautifully decorated with ornamental arches supported by pilasters, above which are oblong panels also intricately carved and flanked by quaint figures. The font has been in use for 500 years, and the communion table dates from the 17th century, as do two beautifully inlaid chairs.

The village is now a conservation area within the new Orton Township, part of Peterborough New Town.

Orwell &

In common with almost every other village in the country, Orwell has changed very much since the Second World War when it was a predominantly agricultural area.

Changes have come in the look of the village. Before the Second World War almost all of the cottages were built of the local chalk known as clunch which from time immemorial had been quarried from the large pit behind the parish church. To preserve it, clunch had to be whitewashed regularly. Therefore Orwell presented a picture, apart from the few houses built of the local 'Cambridge white' brick, of white dwellings covered with thatched roofs. Straw was plentiful and the thatcher lived in the village. Now very few residents can afford to have thatching done and the thatcher would have to be brought in to the village and would probably use Norfolk reeds instead of Orwell straw.

At the time of the Domesday Book, Orwell had 20 people and by 1801 there were 375 inhabitants. The population rose sharply by 1870 to 800 because of the coprolite digging which was carried out quite extensively here and in neighbouring villages.

In 1930 the first council houses were built and they were followed at regular intervals before and after the war by further council building, the last being a quite substantial estate known as Meadowcroft Way, built on what was always known as the Mash, which was a water-logged marsh in 1590.

The church of St Andrew is mostly built of clunch and field stones. The nave and chancel date from about 1200 and the tower is older still. On the south wall of the chancel is a memorial to a rector, Jeremiah Radcliffe, who was one of the translators of the Authorised version of the Bible in 1611.

On St Thomas' Day, a little group of widows, known as 'Goodies' used to call on selected houses for hoped for gifts and would also receive a noble (6s 8d) from the rector. This was left by one of the charities. Another part of the Charity, the Colbatch and Hooper, gave an allowance to apprentices and, in restructured form, still does, as well as giving a generous allowance to those students going on to higher education.

Orwell was one of the most important Congregational (Independent) meeting places in the area in the 17th century but there is not a Congregational or United Reformed church in the village now. In 1959 the Bicentenary of Methodist preaching in the Cambridge Circuit was celebrated in Orwell in the largest barn in the village, at West Farm, which is now converted into dwellings.

Outwell & Upwell 🌿

The villages of Outwell and Upwell are split by the Well Creek, a small river now, but at one time the river Nene flowed through the villages and the area was extremely important. Eventually the Nene was diverted to the course it now follows and the Well Creek gradually became smaller and rather silted up. It is only since the 1960s that the river has been cleared and cleaned out and stocked with fish, done mainly by volunteers who formed the Well Creek Trust.

St Peter's church, with the angels carved in the roof, is illuminated at night and looks really impressive. It is famous for being the model of Dorothy L. Sayers' book *The Nine Tailors*. Behind the church stands Welle Manor with its 'spring', the waters of which are the main ingredient of Norfolk Punch. There are several ghosts at Welle Manor and the present owner is quite willing to tell you about them.

It is pleasant to walk along and see the horse chestnut trees hanging over the river and the foundations of the old blacksmith's which was built right on the very edge of the river. Beside the river are a mixture of old and new houses all blending together giving variety to the scene. In spring the daffodils are out all along the banks, many planted by schoolchildren, many by houseowners who have also planted a variety of trees.

The young of the village enjoy weekly disco's at the Old Mill which has been converted into an hotel. Other organisations also use it as a meeting place. The owners hope to put the sails back onto the mill in the future. The hotel is situated next door to the

Equestrian Centre where international show jumpers come to test themselves and their horses both indoors and out. There is always an event of some kind going on at the Centre.

Every year more and more boats travel up the river passing under the bridge at Outwell which was built in 1682 into the boat basin. There are mooring facilities here and access to the village shops and St Clement's church. In the church is a box with carvings of a boy, girl and twins, called a Churching Box and believed to be the only one of its kind in the country. If a woman gave birth to a girl she would place money into the girl slot, if a boy the boy slot. St Clement's like many other churches these days is fighting to maintain its masonry and timbers.

The river flows beside the church having turned a 90° angle. Originally the river branched here, one branch going to Salters Lode as it does now and one branch going to Wisbech. This course of the river can still be seen although it has been filled in and landscaped to a point.

The Well Creek is the dominant feature in our villages and has been important in the past and with the Leisure industry increasing it is possible that it will be so in the future.

Over

Over is a fenland edge settlement by the river Ouse, 11 miles north west of Cambridge. The name, meaning 'bank of the river', is of Saxon origin. In the Middle Ages, Over was one of the largest villages in Cambridgeshire, with a market place opposite the church.

In 1254 the Bishop of Ely granted a licence to build the church. The stone seats round the wall still exist and this custom originated the phrase 'the weaker go to the wall'. After the porch was added in 1320, it became a meeting place for the villagers. It belonged to Ramsey Abbey until the reign of Henry VIII, when St Mary's church, its tithe and advowson was given to Trinity College, Cambridge. The church has a peel of eight bells, and the only medieval sanctus bell in Cambridgeshire.

Water has ceased to flow through Over church gargoyles, which an East Anglian guide book describes as 'the most engaging gargoyles this side of Notre Dame de Paris'. Rupert Brooke

Over village

obviously did not hold the people of Over in such high esteem as in a poem he wrote 'At Over they fling oaths at one'.

From the 10th century, woad was grown and sold in St Ives market, resulting in the cloth-dyeing industry and glove-making here, and eels and wildfowl were plentiful. Osiers growing by the river were used for basket making. The villagers sabotaged the dykes being built by Vermuyden in 1630 to drain the fens, thinking they would lose their livelihood. Engineers built the Dutch-style houses still to be seen in Fen End and the High Street. Later, meat and dairy products were taken to Cambridge market where, until 1914, Over set the price of butter by the yard.

The Town Hall was built in 1849 for £250 by Over Town Lands Trust on the site of a medieval Guild Hall.

Until 1933 a chain ferry took horses and carts, and later, cars, across the river at Overcote to Needingworth. Now, at weekends, an average of 50 boats go along the river and through the lock worked by the lock keeper. The worst local disaster occurred in 1947 when the river bank burst and hundreds of acres of farmland were flooded. Villagers used to skate on the flooded fen fields, and students came from Cambridge for the sport.

Some houses are built of yellow bricks, hand-made from the mid 19th century to 1931 in Longstanton Road. Many houses were clayed with clay from Mill Pits. The jettied house in West Street was built of wattle and daub, and was the court house.

Some fruit farms remain, growing plums, apples and pears, and nurseries growing pyrethrums and chrysanthemums. Most people commute to Cambridge.

Pampisford ❧

The village lies seven miles south east of Cambridge, and the nearest village is Sawston, which borders it to the north. The river Cam is on the south west boundary, and the Granta to the north east. The eastern boundary of the parish follows the Roman road north of Stumps Cross.

Pampisford grew around its High Street and agriculture was the main activity until the late 18th century. There were two manor houses, both owned by the same family.

In 1840 the Sawby family owned a brewery here, and William was brewer maltster on the site north of Brewery Road. This site was selected for the excellent water found in the area. Latterly malt vinegar was produced at the factory until it closed and was subsequently re-developed.

Pampisford Mill (now a private residence) stands on the river Granta; records show that since at least 1086 a mill has stood on this site. Originally grain was ground here, but in 1802 it was converted into a papermill, although milling of grain may have continued at the same time.

In 1893 the Eastern Counties Leather Company purchased the mill, and £500 was spent converting it into a power source for the leather works. Unfortunately by 1926 the company was in severe financial difficulties, and so Charles Moore (an employee) took it over and revived the business. The firm is still run by the Moore family, now into its fourth generation.

The Dower House (which stands on the High Street) is the only medieval house in the village. When first built this would have been one of the most important buildings. It was probably built in 1455, and may have been the dower house to Sawston Hall.

There are three public houses in Pampisford. The White Horse (near the boundary with Sawston) was completely rebuilt after being demolished in 1937. The Chequers is on the corner of High Street and Brewery Road, and is the oldest pub. Unfortunately in 1973 the thatch caught fire and was replaced by shingles. The Railway Inn is on the northern border near the A11, tucked away on a by-road and opposite Solo park, a re-claimed building materials yard on the site of the old station which closed in 1967.

Parson Drove 🌿

It is reported and generally accepted that the village derives its name from the fact that the parson residing in the neighbouring village of Leverington walked along the mud road or 'drove' to take services in the village church.

There is a hill hidden away where there should be no hill, in an otherwise flat landscape. Legend says it was built by Oliver Cromwell to put his cannon on the top to fire at the old church, or maybe it's a Roman burial place.

Samuel Pepys spent a night at the Swan Inn to visit his relations. Unfortunately his horse was stolen and he was much troubled by gnats. He was later to describe the village in his famous diary as 'a heathen place'.

The focal point of the village is the village green, one of the best to be found in Cambridgeshire. On the green near the Swan Inn is the building known as the cage. It has had many varied uses. It was originally the village lock-up. It was also the village pound and stray animals were kept on the surrounding land. Later it housed the village fire engine. In 1897 to commemorate Queen Victoria's Diamond Jubilee, a clock tower was built onto the roof of the cage. Instead of numbers on the clock faces, letters spell 'VR Sixty Years'. There are two oak trees nearby planted to commemorate the Golden and Diamond jubilees of Queen Victoria's reign. Facing the cage is the village sign which was erected in 1977 to mark Queen Elizabeth II's Silver Jubilee.

The village was the only one in the district to have its own fire engine. The first man to answer the summons to a fire had to catch the horse to pull the engine and there was no shortage of people to man the pumps.

Woad, the plant from which a blue dye was obtained, was grown in the village. The woad mill was demolished in 1917 but there is still a farm called Woad Farm.

Previously the village was self supporting with several shops and tradesmen and was mainly an enclosed community but now the whole village is undergoing a transformation, with many new residents finding the village a friendly place.

On or about August Bank Holiday Monday there is the World Champion Pillow Fight astride a pole across the drain which runs through the village. In the past many has been the time when the local menfolk have held a tug of war across this drain with the referee in a boat on the drain. The highlight was to finish the fight with the sinking of the boat and referee and later ample refreshment at the Swan!

This must be one of the few small villages with two churches. One, going back to the 11th century, is taken care of by the Redundant Churches Trust – but brought to life three times a year. At Christmas it is the scene of a delightful candlelit village carol service.

Peakirk 🌿

The small village of Peakirk, of about 100 houses, lies approximately seven miles north west of Peterborough.

At one end of the village behind Victorian houses, stands a timber workshop founded in 1890, a family firm which makes garden sheds etc. The business is still run by the grandson of the founder. This part of the village is known as the 'new end' as it mainly consists of houses built after the First World War. The solidly built police station is here and a few yards further on, for 31 years, stood the post office, which unfortunately closed in 1987. This building was once the Railway Inn. Behind the post office stands the Victorian station house. The railway line is still open for small diesel trains but the station itself closed in the 1960s.

The older part of the village has many fine stone houses, mostly Georgian. The village pub, the Ruddy Duck, once known as the Black Bull, is now the only surviving public house of three.

Opposite lies the village hall built in 1974 with money raised by the villagers. The monument locally known as the 'Cross' was erected in 1904 by Edward James, a past rector.

By the church stands the 'Chestnuts', a fine square Georgian house often mistaken for the rectory. The parish church dedicated to St Pega is the oldest building in Peakirk, but the foundations of the Hermitage to be found across the village green go back to the mists of time! The rediscovery of the wall paintings in 1949 has brought many visitors to the church. The rector now lives in Glinton and the rectory has become a family home.

The only thatched cottage in Peakirk faces the village green and now belongs to the Wildfowl Trust. The Waterfowl Gardens occupy the site of an old osier bed through which passed the ancient Car Dyke. In Roman times this was one of the chief waterways of East Anglia. Today, however, it is waterfowl which paddle the waterways. Another well known waterway is the Folly Dyke, used by hundreds of fishermen. Crossing the Folly, you leave the parish and encroach onto the black soil of the fens.

Pymoor 🌿

Pymoor is a small village in the parish of Little Downham and lies about six miles north of Ely. The name is spelled Pymore by the GPO, but all the old residents spell it Pymoor.

The land surrounding the village is very black fenland and very rich and fertile. The only grass field in the village is the playing and cricket field. Residents in Pymoor and along the banks of the Hundred Foot river worked mostly on farms, both men and women. In quite recent years the women used to chop the sugar beet out and then chop the ends off it with a curved hook. Some of the men worked on the banks of the river and digging the dykes around the fields. There was also wildfowling and punt gunning in the wash land the other side of the river. Farmers would keep stock on the wash land during the summer, and in the winter these washes took the surplus water and were flooded. The washes stretch from Earith to Denver in Norfolk and are 21 miles long and approximately one mile wide. The RSPB now own about 1850 acres of the washes and the Cambridgeshire Wildlife Trust approximately 250 acres.

Pymoor in years gone by had two or three windmills which were used for draining the land. In later years one windmill ground corn and was also a bakery. The miller had horses and carts going around the village and the outlying farmsteads and cottages delivering the freshly baked bread.

Pymoor had a unique school and church as they were built together in one building under the same roof. The school being at the roadway end, one had to pass through the school to enter the church. This was built out of the village along a public footpath halfway between Pymoor and Oxlode. Sadly Pymoor school, like many village schools was closed on 22nd July 1981. The church struggled on with half the building but was finally closed on Christmas Day 1981.

Close to Pymoor is the Hundred Foot Pumping Engine which pumps the water from the drain into the river. On that spot first stood a windmill, followed by a steam engine, a diesel engine and now the new one driven by electricity. The 'Poet Laureate of the Fens' was born at Pymoor Hill in 1794. He was William Harrison and was well known for many poems, one of which is on the Hundred Foot Pumping Engine today. It reads as follows:

'These Fens have oftimes been by Water drowned
Science a remedy in Water found
The power of Steam she said shall be employed
And the Destroyer by itself destroyed.'

Queen Adelaide 🎐

Queen Adelaide lies to the east of Ely on the B1382. It is a typical long street fen village and although it is quite separate and nearly two miles from Ely itself, it is regarded as being part of the city of Ely.

The village is divided into four by the main railway lines from Ely to Norwich, Peterborough and Kings Lynn which were opened in 1845, 1846 and 1847 respectively.

The present village dates back to the mid 19th century and takes its name from the Queen Adelaide public house which stood near to the river Ouse at the east end of the village. However, there are records of farms and dwellings in the vicinity as far back as AD 970.

Before the fens were drained, the area was covered with many small islands. Turbutsea Island, which was to the south of the present village, was where the monks of Ely landed when they

144

stole the body of Saint Withburga from Dereham in order to bury her next to her sister Saint Etheldreda in Ely Monastery.

The monks would not recognise their island today as the site is covered by a sprawling factory which dominates the skyline of that part of the village. For more than 50 years, during the sugar beet harvest, the road through the village throbbed with the noise of tractor and lorry engines taking the raw beet to be processed, and the sickly, sweet smell hung heavily in the air over the village. Today the workers' houses have fallen down, the smell has gone and the factory has become a storage and distribution centre. Lorries still thunder down the main street of the village though, carrying their loads of Fen potatoes, carrots and onions destined for the markets of the Midlands.

The river provides excellent fishing and is also used by the Cambridge University boat club for practice. A notable event was the 1944 Boat Race between Oxford and Cambridge. It was thought to be too dangerous to hold the race in London during the war so the stretch of river between Littleport bridge and Queen Adelaide bridge was used. Five thousand people watched Oxford win by three quarters of a length.

At one time Queen Adelaide, like most villages had a school, a shop and a church. Now these are all private houses. The church, dedicated to Saint Etheldreda was erected in 1883 to replace a mission church. Standing as it does near the river, it was not unknown for couples to travel by boat to church to be married. It was closed in about 1968.

Ramsey ✤

Ramsey stands on what was once an island in the fens, equidistant from Huntingdon and Peterborough. It is growing fast with new housing estates everywhere and many commuters travelling as far as London. Newcomers find it a very friendly place.

Ramsey church is a fine Norman building, with the 14 arches of its long nave on splendid pillars, no two pairs alike. Its most precious historic possession is probably the oak lectern used by the monks in the great days of the abbey. The old abbey is now a splendid secondary school. Many old buildings in Ramsey were destroyed in the Great Fire of the 18th century, but the ruins of the abbey gateway are now in the care of the National Trust. It houses an effigy of Duke Ailwyn, Alderman of all England.

The Cromwells had many connections with Ramsey. Several entries in the church registers refer to them, the earliest dated 1559. William, Oliver's cousin, is believed to have been innocently responsible for bringing the plague to Ramsey on a piece of cloth from London in 1666. It resulted in the deaths of 400 people, including himself and his family.

A dummy clock stands in the wide central street, the Great Whyte. It was erected in 1888 'To the Honoured Memory of the Right Honourable Edward Fellowes 1st Baron of Ramsey'.

Sawston

The earliest record of the village of Sawston is found in Saxon times when there was a settlement called Salsingtune. By Domesday (1086) the village had three manors and 125 people.

Sawston's most notable historic event happened in 1553 when Princess Mary, soon to be queen, stayed the night at Sawston Hall when being pursued by her enemies. Tradition has it that she set out the next day dressed as a dairymaid riding behind her protector John Huddleston, the owner of Sawston Hall. On reaching high ground they looked back and saw flames and smoke rising from the hall which had been fired by the Protestant mob. The hall was badly damaged and later John Huddleston was granted material from the ruins of Cambridge castle with which to rebuild his home. This Tudor mansion built in 1557 (with a priest hole and the traditional ghost!) is still standing today and is now a language school.

Many notable buildings remain from early days – Brook House the oldest of all dates from the 13th century, the Queen's Head pub from the 15th century and Ward House from the 16th century. Parts of the parish church date back to Norman times.

A custom from the 16th century has been upheld almost to the present day. This was a charity, instigated in his will by John Huntingdon, that every year two acres of his land should be sown with peas for the relief of the poor people in the village. The picking of the peas was allocated to a certain time on a certain day when the poor and needy would line the field. Nowadays the 'poor and needy' line the fields armed with plastic dustbin bags and take home the peas to fill their freezers!

Agriculture was naturally the main occupation of Sawston folk but in the 19th century Sawston expanded into an industrial village as many local industries were set up. The first successful business was the tannery set up by Thomas Evans, whose son later introduced the manufacture of chamois leather. Then came John Crampton who installed a printing works behind his shop. Edward Towgood, another big name, owned the paper mill and gained a wide reputation for the manufacture of the finest grades of paper. These industries are still very much alive today and account for a large proportion of the jobs available in the village. There is also an expanding industrial estate.

Sawston was the first village in England to have a village college, introduced by the educationalist Henry Morris. Many of the village activities centre round the village college which also has a wide adult education programme.

There is as yet no village hall, though one has been talked about for well over a hundred years! There is no cinema and no market but there is a health centre, a fire station, three churches, a good shopping centre and a more than adequate number of pubs! Although there is a tendency for villages to become dormitories for the nearest large town or city Sawston has maintained and is increasing its own identity and has indeed become a centre itself for many smaller surrounding villages.

Sawtry ✑

Sawtry is situated just off the A1, between Peterborough and Huntingdon. In the 1930s it was a quiet, rural village.

The school was situated at the top of the hill and all ages of children attended there, from 5 years to 14 years. There was a bell on the top of the school and every morning at about ten minutes to nine, it was rung by the boys in the top class.

A little further on stood the Methodist chapel and, after passing a few houses and the butcher's shop, one came to the village green. Every year early in June a gathering was held on the green. It took the form of a procession and a brass band, followed by a service in the church. The collection taken at the church was given to local hospitals. All the following week a fair was held on the green.

After the Second World War the housing estates began to be built and altered Sawtry completely, from a straggling village of about 500 inhabitants to a village that is almost a town of 5,000 people.

The village college was built in 1963 and a new infant school in 1972, in the field opposite the old school. A swimming pool was also built in 1972. Then in 1982 a new junior school was built and the old school was bought by the Parish Council. Sawtry has many more shops now and the WI hold a market every Friday, selling home made food and vegetables and fruit that is in season.

Shepreth 🐾

Shepreth is an attractive village of about 250 houses, lying eight miles south of Cambridge, next to the A10. The small river Shep makes an attractive feature as it wanders through the parish, to the delight of the fishing-inclined children. The younger children enjoy feeding the ducks. The southern parish boundary runs along Guilden Brook, which, like the river Shep runs into the river Cam.

Earlier inhabitants of Shepreth must have been energetic and enjoyed visiting neighbours as they established footpaths to all the nearby villages! These offer pleasant walks, often near the rivers. One runs from opposite the Green Man at the top of Frog End (beyond the bypass) up the 'Nave', along the river to the Fowlmere RSPB Reserve. A nave is the square in the centre of a cartwheel, and that was the size of pipe that was used to divert water from the river Shep along a ditch which ran past the houses in Frog End and can still be seen most of the way. This used to supply the cottages with water for all their needs except drinking; that had to be fetched from one of the three village pumps. The nearest pump has had to be moved to make room for the by-pass.

The cottages on the north side of Frog End road (which used to be over-run with frogs which reputedly sang as sweetly as larks in the night air in summer!) are mostly built end-on to the road as the land was divided into narrow strips following the Enclosure Act in 1823. The pattern of these can still be seen, although it is beginning to change as some of the back land is sold.

The village has a rich variety of houses, the small new groups blending happily with the traditional lath and plaster timber framed houses so typical of Cambridgeshire. Roofs are varied and may be of thatch, tile or slate. Two mills which used to grind corn, powered by the Shep when it had a bigger flow of water, have been converted to houses.

The church, in a beautifully kept churchyard, is tucked away at the end of the High Street. It dates from Norman times with most of the following centuries leaving their mark. Local clunch and flint have been used in its walls as well as bricks, stone and cement.

If you turn into the village from the A10 through a beautiful avenue of beech trees, you can see one of the large pits, now filled with water. The pits were dug to provide chalk for use in the making of cement. The East Anglian Cement Company pit down Angle Lane provided a specialized cement that matched old mortar and was made specifically for the repair of old buildings, especially churches, including St Paul's Cathedral in London.

Soham 🌿

Until the draining of the fens a huge mere existed between Soham and Ely, the local people relying largely on fishing for their food and income. King Canute is known to have crossed the mere en route for the monastic establishment at Ely.

The present day Soham has a population of about 8,000 and it is situated midway between Ely and Newmarket and approximately 20 miles from Cambridge. At first sight it might be thought that there is little of interest in Soham but closer investigation reveals a wealth of old houses, some dating back to the 17th century. On one old inn, now a house, can still be seen the painted sign 'Licensed to let a horse and gig'.

The history of Soham goes back to at least the Bronze and Iron Age. Aerial photography and digs have revealed evidence of occupation during these periods. Whilst there is little sign of Roman occupation some artefacts of the period have been found. Of the Anglo Saxon time a little more is known. Three cemeteries have been traced – one in the centre of Soham and two others on the Fordham side. In about AD 650 a monastery was founded in Soham by St Felix but it was sacked by the Danes in AD 870 and never rebuilt. In the fine parish church of St Andrew, traces of a painting on the north chancel wall are thought to be of St Felix in his vestments.

The present church dates back to the 12th century and amongst some of its many interesting features are a beautiful hammerbeam roof with carved figures, carved poppy ends to some of the old benches, a fine transitional Norman arch, and good examples of fairly modern stained glass including one window dedicated to William Case Morris, an Ely man educated in Soham who later became the 'Dr Barnado' of Argentina. The tower contains a peal of ten bells which is well known to ringers throughout Cambridgeshire and much further afield. Outside the north porch is an interesting tomb commemorating Mary D'Aye, the great granddaughter of Oliver Cromwell.

Opposite the main entrance to the church is the 500 year old Fountain Inn which in former times was used for Court purposes and meetings of the local Justices. Although much of the public house was destroyed by fire in 1900 part of a panelled room, complete with a shield and coat of arms of Roger de Torel, dated 1533, still forms part of the present public lounge. Outside the inn, overhanging the road, is one of only two or three steelyards left in the country. This one is 3–400 years old and was used for weighing agricultural produce from pounds in weight to tons.

On the 2nd June 1944 Soham was almost destroyed when an ammunition train caught fire but the village was saved by the bravery of Fireman J. W. Nightall, GC (killed) and Driver B. Gimbert, GC (badly injured), who detached the blazing wagon, and also the devotion to duty of Signalman F. Bridges (killed) and Guard H. Clarke who was severely shocked.

At the present time Soham is a thriving community. Although individual farm owners still play a big part in the local economy there are also a number of large firms in the district. Added to this are two industrial estates where a wide variety of items are made which help to contribute to the wealth and employment of the district. Many local firms contributed to the setting up of the Soham and District Sports Centre which is now self supporting and extensively used by people of all ages.

Somersham ✒

This large village situated on the edge of the fens is in a mainly fruit growing area. Over recent years it has grown and is still growing rapidly.

Somersham was recorded in the Domesday Book in 1086 and may have been visited by Hereward the Wake when fleeing from the Normans.

The Parish Church is said to stand on the remains of a 7th century wooden church that was built when the Kingdom of Mercia became Christian following the death of Penda.

During the 18th century the Somersham Spa waters were famous for health giving properties. In 1815 there was a terrible fire that destroyed much of the village of that time.

Today the ever growing population is well provided for day to day requirements with a number of shops that provide basic needs. There are also schools, three churches, health centre, four public houses and a social club. Many organisations exist for all ages, interests and sporting activities. The village also boasts of its Town Band and the privately owned local museum. In all, a very active and caring community.

Stapleford ✤

Stapleford's village sign, which was erected to commemorate Elizabeth II's Silver Jubilee, depicts, among other things, the stapol or white post which marked the ford across the nearby river Granta.

Some of the older buildings in Stapleford include Stapleford Hall, a large thatched 17th century building and, at the other end of the social scale, Dormer Cottage, a small house dating back 300 years. Middlefield House, designed by Lutyens and built in 1908 is a notable example of a later style of architecture. The Slaughterhouse, a small thatched building dating back to c1840, was originally the property of Mr Barker, a butcher of Stapleford. Next to it stand two attractive cottages restored by the Cambridgeshire Cottage Improvement Society in 1977.

St Andrew's church has been considerably altered and extended over the centuries, but its oldest surviving part is the Norman chancel arch. There is evidence of church bells in 1524 when 60 lambs were bequeathed to pay for a frame for them. All five bells were restored in 1911 and a sixth one added. Improvements to the church continue all the time. Substantial internal reorganisation, including the building of a new organ, has taken place in the 1980s.

One vicar, William Lee (d.1617) gave his house and land at Stapleford to the church and the poor. He is commemorated in a brass in the church. Another incumbent was Rev. C. H. T. W.

Stapleford village sign

Daw, who died in 1897 and stated in his will that his right leg was to be sawn off by two surgeons so that he could fit into an ordinary sized coffin! A certificate was to be signed by the surgeons to the effect that they had carried out the work and they were to be paid three guineas each or take the limb in part payment if they so desired.

Stapleford Community School is still a thriving centre for community life in the village. It was opened in 1878 and the original red brick building still forms part of the present school, although it has been extended to many times its original size. The original schoolhouse was converted to a hostel for pupils of the adjacent Green Hedges School for handicapped children. This school and its pupils are taken very much to heart by the people of Stapleford and receive constant generous help and support from them.

The parish of Stapleford includes Wandlebury ring, a hill fort dating back to the 3rd century BC. Formerly the property of the Dukes of Leeds, Wandlebury is now a nature reserve and as such has many visitors from all over the county who enjoy walks, birdwatching or simply sitting in the sun. The Godolphin Arabian, one of the three horses from which all British racing stock is descended, is buried at Wandlebury.

Stetchworth 🐴

Stetchworth lies between Newmarket and Cambridge. The Devil's Dyke runs very close to the village, which has existed as a village since the 11th century. It presently has a population of about 600.

Formerly the inhabitants of Stetchworth were employed in agriculture and in providing local services. Nowadays they work in Cambridge and elsewhere, although stud farms still provide employment on the land. The National Stud lies within Stetchworth's boundaries and other local stud farms are the Egerton Stud, the Collin Stud and the Stetchworth Park Stud. The Marquis of Granby is the only remaining public house; the Live and Let Live has been converted to an hotel, and the White Horse Hotel is now a private house. There is still a post office and several travelling shops visit the village.

A part-time general store run by volunteers is housed in the Ellesmere Centre, a multi-purpose building opened in 1984 to extend and complement the Ellesmere Hall. The new building provides sports facilities and accommodation for many clubs and classes. It was designed for use by the parishes of Stetchworth, Woodditton, Dullingham, Kirtling, Westley Waterless, Brinkley and Burrough Green. It is one of only three such centres in the country, set up by the Development Commission to improve the standard of rural life.

Lord Gorges, the Superintendent and Surveyor General of the corporation which drained the Great or Bedford level, lived in Stetchworth and in the north aisle of the nave of Stetchworth church there is a large monument to Henry, his son who died in 1674 aged 19.

Graffiti is not new. Two pillars in the north side of the nave have medieval figures scratched on them. Thought to have been drawn to record a visit to Stetchworth by Queen Philippa, they depict a woman wearing an elaborate headdress of gold wire, an owl with a similar headdress, a man, a cat and a type of wader bird – a common sight before the fens were drained.

Mill Lane found fame in 1981 when a young family discovered treasure buried beneath their pantry floor. They found gold sovereigns and half sovereigns with a face value of £100, valued today at £40,000, dating from 1818–1825. A treasure trove enquiry was held but the coins were returned to the finders.

People say that, because of the high incidence of disease, Stetchworth was one of the first villages locally to be connected to the mains sewer. The need for an efficient sewer may have given rise to Dullingham's epithet for the village – 'stinking Stetchworth'. The Alley, a narrow lane off the High Street, was formerly known more colourfully as 'Turd Alley' for at the end of the Alley villagers without modern sanitation used to empty the buckets from their privies!

Stibbington & Wansford 🦢

The village of Stibbington was originally part of the Roman town of Durobrivæ, and there are still Roman kilns in the corner of the field by a small council estate called Roman Drive. The village meandered along the Great North Road, the boundary being the river Nene. A lane passes by the church of St John the Baptist to the river, and there used to be a ford across to the village of Sutton. The river was the ecclesiastical boundary between the villages of

Stibbington and Wansford until 1976, when the lower portion was joined to Wansford for ecclesiastical purposes only. The jurisdiction of the Stibbington Parish Council however, still remains to half way across the bridge. The village of Stibbington was completely bisected by the dual carriageway of the A1 when it was built and the part which contains The Haycock and the local shops is now commonly and erroneously known as Wansford.

The village of Stibbington formerly had the services of the following: two bakeries, a blacksmith, two wheelwrights, a saddler, a tailor, a stationer, a butcher, a post office, three grocery shops and two schools. One of these was the Wansford School for Young Ladies, which was situated at Barnaby House. Now there remains only one grocery cum post office and Wingrove's butcher's shop.

The Haycock Hotel was a famous coaching inn and parts of the present building are thought to date back to the 13th century. It was originally called The Swan but was renamed The Haycock in the 18th century. Post horses were kept here for travellers journeying on the Great North Road and Queen Victoria spent the night at this hotel two years before she ascended the throne.

During the 18th and early 19th centuries, Wansford had a paper making industry which was situated in the grounds now known as Stibbington House. The only reminder today of the paper making mills is a public house called The Paper Mills.

The church, dedicated to St Mary, part of which was built in Saxon times, stands on a hill looking down over the slowly meandering river Nene.

There has been a crossing over the river probably since the Domesday Book was compiled. In 1571, three arches of the wooden bridge were destroyed in a flood. Wansford has three bridges. The oldest bridge was built in the 16th century and links the village of Wansford with the parish of Stibbington. The third bridge was built across the river near the Mermaid Inn, about 1975 when the A1 was developed into a dual carriageway.

Wansford was once important as a river port and has interesting old associations. Less than a century ago, a quaint old flagstone quay presented a busy sight, where cargoes of coal, wheat and other grain were loaded and unloaded.

The river is a popular haunt for anglers. Walking along the river in summer, you'll find a number of cabin cruisers berthed by the old bridge.

A nearby attraction is the Nene Valley Railway, which is run by a Steam Preservation Society and is a standard gauge steam railway, running from Wansford Station in Stibbington to Peterborough N.V.R. Station, via Ferry Meadows and Orton Mere.

Stilton 🌿

Nearly 2,000 years ago the Roman legions marched along Ermine Street on the road that was later to become one of Britain's busiest thoroughfares – the Great North Road.

Two hundred and fifty years ago, travellers were still using the same route, stopping at the many posting houses in the village. One traveller, Lord Harley, is reputed to have stopped at The Bell Inn, which was already over 200 years old, and sampled the unusual cheese said to have been made in Stilton. He was not impressed! Nevertheless Stilton cheese, although no longer made in the area, continues to be one of the country's most popular cheeses and is often called 'The King of English cheese'.

Today, the travellers are replaced by tourists trying to find the 'cheese factory'. Though unsuccessful in this, their visits are not in vain, for the ancient Bell and Angel still stand picturesquely commanding the village centre, with its ancient pump. Not far away stands the church of Saint Mary Magdalene, with its 13th century nave arcades and 15th century font.

To the north is Norman Cross, where the old mail coaches from Peterborough and Lincoln joined the Great North Road. This is also the site of the Norman Cross prisoner-of-war camp, where French and Dutch prisoners were housed during the Napoleonic Wars. All that remains of this period is a large white house – the former Governor's residence.

Nearby, on the side of the A1 is a column surmounted by a spread eagle, a memorial to 1,770 French soldiers who died whilst in captivity. Ironically the memorial was unveiled in July 1914, just a few days before the 'war to end all wars' began.

Not all the prisoners returned to their homeland at the end of the Napoleonic Wars as can be seen by the many Anglicized French names found amongst the local population.

A different kind of 'invasion' followed in the 1940s, when American servicemen came to operate from the many wartime airfields that criss-crossed East Anglia. 'Yanks' were billeted at

Stilton and an elderly inhabitant remembers village housewives taking in 'American washing' and several young ladies leaving as GI brides.

Stilton still retains links with the Americans as many families from the nearby USAF base at Alconbury live in the village.

Since the Stilton by pass was opened in 1958, the continuous A1 traffic no longer divides the village and relative peace has returned. However, Stilton still bustles with a rising population which now stands at about 2,000.

There is an annual event, known as 'Cheese Rolling'. In this keenly contested race, teams from all the surrounding area, many in fancy dress, bowl a 'cheese' (a large log sawn from a telegraph pole and painted to look like a Stilton cheese) along the High Street. The winning team is awarded a crate of beer and a whole Stilton cheese. The street is lined with stalls, increasing the fair-like atmosphere whilst, at the same time, raising money for charity.

Stow cum Quy 🍃

Originally two settlements, Stow and Quy were regarded as one village as early as the 1086 Domesday Book. Locally it is known as Quy (but never as Stow).

Stow means a 'holy place' and, although only some 17 metres above sea level, it stands up above the surrounding fenland. It is thought that the Saxon church built here was on an earlier pagan site. Only the fragment of a Saxon arch can be seen in the present church, rebuilt in 1340, which stands on the edge of the village next to the busy Quy interchange on the Cambridge bypass.

Stow Manor, long since disappeared, was inhabited by the D'Engayne family until 1367. The last 'Lady Gains', perhaps desolate at having no children, is said still to walk the river bank, hung about with chains, beckoning and promising to show any who dare follow where she has buried treasure.

Quy comes from the Anglo Saxon words for 'Cow Isle' but 'we're whully lazy hereabouts and now tha's jest plain Quy'. Quy also had its own church, St Nicholas, near the crossroads in the centre of the village. Evidently it had been in ruins for so long that the story grew up that Quy people wanted a church but as fast as they built up the walls the Devil came and pulled them down again overnight so that Quy did not get a church.

Quy Hall belonged to the Martin family, the London bankers, from 1720 to 1854. Clement Francis, a Cambridge solicitor with a large family, bought the property in 1854 and the house was partly rebuilt and restored to its earlier appearance by the London architect W. White in 1868–70. The Francis family still own Quy estate. At the end of the last war they owned 70% of the houses in Quy; since then there have been council and private houses built and some of the older properties have been sold though some 30% of the housing is still part of the estate.

In February the shrubbery, the island in the grounds, and the surrounding woodland are a carpet of white snowdrops and golden aconites amidst the dark green ivy leaves. For some 75 years the Francis family have allowed the snowdrops to be picked for specific charities beginning with bunches sent to London by train to raise funds for the Red Cross in the First World War, up to the present day when a gallant band of ladies brave the icy winds picking 3,000 bunches for sale by Cambridge florists for church funds.

At the southern edge of the village are 70 acres of Quy Fen over which Quy, Horningsea and Fen Ditton have equal rights. Now the fen is let for grazing and the income is shared by the villages. In olden times all parishioners had the right to cut hay or peasticks, but no animals were allowed to graze there. There is a memorial stone to William Ison, aged 29, who was struck by lightning when cutting hay in 1873. In the late 1880s, Mrs Francis as lady of the manor, gave permission for coprolites to be dug in Quy Fen in order to provide work for local people. Work was carried on for about four years but the company was wound up in debt and the last of the 'cuts' were left to fill with water instead of being filled in. The largest cut in Quy Fen has since then always been popular with swimmers, though tragically at least two people have been drowned there. The area round the cut has rare fen plants, is a breeding ground for dragonflies and damselflies and has thus been designated a Site of Special Scientific Interest.

Stretham ✤

The village of Stretham lies just off the A10, a few miles to the south of Ely. The name is derived from the old Roman road,

Akeman Street, but it is thought that there was a settlement here long before Roman times.

The most famous local landmark is Stretham Old Engine, built in the 1830s to drain the fens. Its 37 ft waterwheel used to lift 30 tons of water at one turn, draining it into a river flowing above. You can imagine the size of the machinery needed for this task. It is all still there, beautifully preserved, seemingly ready to chug into action and well worth a visit.

On the left hand side of the street going north out of the village stands the high, handsome, black Tower Windmill, which looks across the countryside to where Ely Cathedral floats in majesty on the fens.

In the village, St James' church has a 14th century tower and some other medieval work, but was thoroughly restored by the Victorians. A fine 15th century cross stands in the centre of Stretham, surrounded by the church, the Red Lion, the Chequers Inn, the post office and the Spaceward Recording Studios. The Spaceward Studios are cunningly disguised as the old village school and are said to contain more futuristic equipment than Dr Who's old blue police box!

Stuntney

Stuntney is a tiny place now but in the past it has had a place in history. When Hereward the Wake was defending Ely against the Normans, Stuntney was one of the bridgeheads of the Norman attack .A few hundred years later Stuntney laid another claim to fame as the home of Oliver Cromwell's mother, one of the Steward family, at the little Elizabethan manor – Stuntney Hall – which stood on Hall Hill. Steward Close is named after the family.

The most important and probably the oldest building in Stuntney is the church of the Holy Cross, with its Saxon origins. It has two well preserved chevron arches, one around the entrance door on the south side and another inside the church, and these are good examples of Norman architecture.

Visitors to the village today notice the beautiful village sign with its shire horse, which was made for the village by local craftsmen. Stuntney has a long association with the shire horse. Before the advent of the steam traction engine and the tractor, the horse was the most important source of power on the land at Cole Ambrose

Farm in Stuntney and around the turn of the century there were about 200 horses, shires and hackneys, on the farm. Cole Ambrose was the founder member of the Shire Horse Society and one of the leading breeders in the country.

These horses can still be seen in the village today although they are no longer worked. They are the responsibility of Mr 'Dekker' Murfitt.

The village 'pound' was an important feature during the days when many farm animals or horses strayed from their owners, and were kept in the pound until they were claimed. The keeper of the pound was obliged to receive any animals offered into his custody. Today the pound forms part of the property Anchor House, once a public house and now a charming private house.

The most macabre relic of all was probably the tomb which was found by men sub-soiling the land at Thorney Hill. The tomb contained a skeleton which was taken to Ely museum where it can still be seen today.

Although many features of village life have disappeared, there is one old custom which has been revived and that is the ancient ceremony of 'beating the bounds' which takes place at Rogation-tide just before Ascension Day. A procession from the church headed by the priest, a server bearing a crucifix and parishioners carrying willow wands, stop at various well known points along the parish boundary to beat the bounds. Hymns are sung and prayers said to ask for a good harvest. Although Stuntney is a tiny village the boundary is very extensive so nowadays stopping points are limited, and the opportunity is taken to combine this ceremony with a picnic outing.

Sutton ✎

Sutton, a village situated half a mile south of the A47, between Wansford and Castor, has 43 houses and all but four of the original cottages have been modernised.

The manor house of Sutton is The Grange, built in the 17th century. It was owned by the Ecclesiastical Commissioners and sold by them to the Rev. Hopkinson in 1898, whose descendant still lives there. The church, dedicated to St Michael and All Angels, was originally dedicated to St Giles, the patron saint of cripples, lepers and nursing mothers. It was built early in the 12th century and only the chancel arch supports survive, but much 13th century work remains. The church was largely rebuilt in 1867–8 out of the proceeds of the sale of land at Sutton Heath for the building of the Wansford branch railway.

West of the church, the road has become an overgrown muddy track to the river Nene. There was a ford across to Stibbington, but it was unused for some time and it was finally destroyed by dredging in the 1950s to permit river traffic.

The farm, Manor Farm, is 17th century, and the somewhat derelict 18th century cottage opposite was originally the Cross Keys public house.

Sutton village is now a designated conservation area. The site of the old Roman road Ermine Street, which ran from London to Lincoln is to the east of the village at the site of the Sutton Cross, which is the junction point of the parish boundaries of Sutton, Upton and Ailsworth.

Sutton (nr Ely) 🐝

Sutton lies on a ridge of land at the south west edge of the Isle of Ely, so that the church of St Andrew rises tall on the skyline over the village, with its memorable 14th century tower. The church itself is spacious and beautiful, well worth seeing.

Every two years Mr Peter Gimbert opens his house in the High Street to visitors. The house is over 250 years old and behind it, in a large barn, John Wesley first preached in Sutton in 1774. The owner of the house at that time was Clemence Tubbs, Wesley's host. Tubbs took him on the next stage of his journey, carrying him on the back of his horse and having to go through flooded land to Earith. Relics of John Wesley still exist in the village.

Next door to Mr Tubbs lived some Quakers, in a house which is still standing. The garden of their house was used as a Quaker burial ground.

Approximately two miles from Sutton there was once a monastery. From there, legend has it that a tunnel ran, connecting it with the village church. The tunnel is blocked now but the entrance is still there.

Many new houses have been built in Sutton over the past few years, but it is not always a straightforward process to bring the modern world into an ancient village. When one new house was occupied, trouble with the drains soon followed. A long saga of plumbers, council roadmen and parties of workmen began. At last, the old man who had lived next door for decades and had been watching all the goings-on, asked the foreman if he would like to know where the water from the house was going, since it did not seem to be appearing anywhere where it should. He led them across the road, down a drove some 60 or 70 yards and triumphantly showed them the water running out of an old drainpipe into a ditch between two fields, an ancient disused drain which the professionals knew nothing about. Sometimes a little local knowledge is a marvellous thing!

Swaffham Bulbeck ✍

Swaffham Bulbeck, and its hamlet Commercial End, is situated at the head of an artificial waterway or 'lode' approximately seven miles north east of Cambridge.

There are several interesting buildings still intact. Burgh Hall, once one of three manors, is a richly timbered 'Wealden style' house, now a farm. Lordship Cottage, identified as a 13th century one cell chapel, with Tudor additions. The 'Abbey' was founded in the late 12th century by Isabel de Bolebec as a Benedictine Priory for nuns. Never a rich foundation, it was surrendered by the last prioress Joan Spilman at the Dissolution of the Monasteries in 1536. It is reputed that she liked the neighbourhood so much that she remained in a cave in the vicarage garden for at least a year afterwards. Today, the vaulted undercroft is all that remains, with an 18th century home built above it.

The church of St Mary is mainly 14th century with an earlier tower. There are some interesting carved bench ends within.

The Rev. Leonard Jenyns (1828–1849) was perhaps the most notable vicar of the village. An ardent botanist, he was proposed as botanist to accompany Captain Fitzroy on the *Beagle* but refused and proposed instead his friend Charles Darwin.

There is also a Free Church in Commercial End. The Free Church Society was formed in 1899 and their first chapel was known as 'The Tin Tabernacle'. An appeal was launched for funds for a permanent chapel which was finally opened in 1926.

Although farming was the dominant feature, the village was not entirely reliant upon it. The fen itself had provided peat cutting and reed cutting. Saffron had been grown reasonably successfully for a time. With the draining of the fen during the late 17th century a navigable route was opened to Commercial End (or Newnham as it was known). Wharves were built and a trading establishment began which reached its peak in the early 19th century under Thomas Bowyer – sending out agricultural produce and importing coal and wines etc. The water trade was eventually killed by the railway, but the unique appearance of Commercial End today is the legacy that Bowyer left.

Village life has changed much since then. In 1851 the population supported three shopkeepers, two shoemakers, two cornmillers, three carpenters, two wheelwrights, a harnessmaker, bricklayers and shepherds as well as five public houses plus other beer sellers. Today there are only two public houses and a shop cum post-office.

Education in the village came via two gifts of money in 1710 and 1722 to found a charity school for the poor children. The new National School was opened in 1874 and is still in use today.

All was not hard work. At the beginning of the 20th century a wife sale was recorded as having taken place at the Royal Oak. Villagers were amused when two tinkers arrived, one of whom offered his wife for sale at auction. She was finally sold for half-a-crown to his companion!

Swavesey ✑

Swavesey is a fen edge village, eight miles west of Camrbidge. It lies between the Via Devana (A604) to the south, and the river Great Ouse to the north.

At the north end of the village, on the edge of the fen, stands the fine parish church of St Andrew, which is mainly of the 13th and 14th centuries although there is evidence of an earlier Saxon building in the stonework of the present building. By the middle of the 19th century the church was in a very dilapidated state, and in 1867 extensive restoration work was carried out which has resulted in the beautiful church we have today.

Adjoining the church is the site of the priory which was founded by Count Alan of Brittany, who granted the church of Swavesey and its offering to the Benedictine Abbey of Saints Sergius and Bacchus at Angers. Earthworks still remain in this area, and aerial photographs indicate the priory covered quite a large area.

Near to the church is the vicarage, which was built in 1863 and was used by the vicar of Swavesey until quite recently, and also the charming manor house, which in the 16th century belonged to the Cutts family.

As well as the priory and a castle, of which earthworks still remain, Swavesey was also a market town. A market and fair was granted by Henry III to Alan de la Zouch in 1244, and it would seem that at that time he was trying to develop the village into a thriving commercial centre with boats using the dock in Market Street. Although we have no records when the market ceased to operate, the name Market Street still survives and remains of the dock were visible until quite recently.

Although through the years Swavesey has lost many of its houses by fire, a few interesting ones have survived including Ryder's Farm, which has been dated back to 1280, No 10 High Street the old market house which dates from the late 17th century, and the White Horse, the one remaining public house in the village. In 1913 Swavesey suffered its most disastrous fire, when in March that year on a very windy day, 26 thatched houses in Station Road were burnt down in 1½ hours, and over 100 people were made homeless.

In 1920, Mr Reginald Barwell came to the village and bought the 'Old House', with the farmyard and buildings, and for a time became a poultry farmer, but in 1927 he started the Barwell Tyre Renewing Co in the redundant farm buildings. The firm continued to expand, and in 1969 and 1973 the Barwell Machine and Rubber Group Ltd, as it was then called, received the Queen's Award to Industry for Export Achievement, so from quite small beginnings it became a major employer in the village.

Although Swavesey, a few years ago, could rightly be described as an agricultural village, many changes have taken place since 1945. Whitton Close, Carters Way, Priory Avenue and Thistle Green have all been built. Many sites where houses stood in the last century have been built on again and 1958 saw the building of the village college to serve this village and the surrounding area.

Thorney

Until 1910 Thorney village and the parish comprising over 40,000 acres was included in the estate of the Duke of Bedford. He had received the area of Thorney as a gift from a grateful sovereign in recognition of the Duke's labours in draining the fens. After 1910 the estate was sold to the tenant farmers for in many cases, as little as ten shillings an acre.

The incumbency of the Abbey remained in the gift of the Duke during the lifetime of the vicar, the Reverend W. Symont. As there were three other places where Anglican services were held it was necessary to have a curate. His stipend was the responsibility of the parishioners and to this end an annual tea and concert was held in the Abbey Rooms. The local farmers' wives brought their finest crockery and each catered for one table. They provided huge quantities of food to the great enjoyment of all!

Throughout the years of the close dependence on the Duke of Bedford and also after the dispersal of the estate, the people of Thorney had learnt to be self sufficient in many ways. Under the auspices of the Duke many craftsmen had flourished, including carpenters, wheelwrights, blacksmiths, millers, builders and bakers. When the farmers became landowners there entered into the whole community a sense of competition. Clubs were formed and cricket, football, bowls and tennis were played in season. A shire horse and foal show was held annually on the first Thursday in June and a Flower Show attracted a lot of support.

At that time there was a large acreage of grass and vast quantities of beef cattle and sheep were raised. Many horses and foals were reared in strong competition with neighbouring farmers. Some of these horses were commandeered by the Ministry of War for hauling guns to the battlefields in France during the First World War. One farmer exported some of his fine animals to the American state of Illinois where four brothers by the name of Truman carried on extensive farming. These men were related to a man of the same name who subsequently became President of the USA.

The majority of the grassland was put to the plough during the Second World War when the National War Effort demanded the maximum production of food. These solid countrymen rose to the occasion with unstinted zeal and helped to fill the nation's larder in an hour of desperate need.

Thornhaugh 🌿

Thornhaugh village lies west of the A1, nine miles north west of Peterborough. Its name is derived from the Anglo Saxon and means a thorn enclosed low-lying meadow beside a stream. There is evidence of a settlement as far back as the 12th century and for many centuries, the population would have consisted of land-owners, farmers, clergymen, millers and workers on the land, in the woods and quarries. Thornhaugh is a village with a small static population but the area within the parish is one of the largest in the county of Cambridgeshire. Nowadays there is no shop, no school, no public house or bus service within the village but it has great character and beauty to compensate for the lack of facilities. It was declared a conservation area in 1979.

St Andrew's church contains a monument to the memory of Sir William Russell, First Baron Russell of Thornhaugh. He is recorded as holding high office in the service of Queen Elizabeth I and was a comrade-in-arms and close friend of Sir Philip Sidney. Sir Philip bequeathed to Sir William Russell his suit of gilded armour and many people thought that the helmet which was displayed for many years above the monument in the church, was part of this armour. Although this was not so, the helmet was nevertheless found to be of great value and was promptly removed for safe keeping.

Sacrewell Mill, now part of Sacrewell Farm, lies half a mile to the east of the Great North Road in the north east angle of the junction between the A1 and the A47. The mill stream forms the boundary between the parishes of Thornhaugh and Wansford. Sacrewell Mill, as it now stands, dates from about the middle of the 18th century; a stone in the north west corner of the main building bears the date 1755. It is likely however, that the mill had several predecessors, as there are remains of three substantial Romano-British villas on Sacrewell Farm, showing evidence of grain drying and malting. It is thought that the Romans intro-duced the watermill.

Sacrewell is steeped in history and the farm probably derives its name from a very strong spring which rises in one of the fields. There have been many dwellers at Sacrewell for hundreds of years. Neolithic implements have been found and there are several prehistoric circles of uncertain date and use. In Roman times the farm probably supplied food for the industrial population based on Castor and Nene valley potteries. Weapons, tools of flint and Roman pottery are still found, which dates the buildings at about AD 300.

Thriplow

The small village of Thriplow sits astride the Icknield Way, eight miles south of Cambridge, and is pronounced Triplow; the 'h' being added much later.

Today the village boasts a shop, a school, a pub, a bus service into Cambridge and a cricket meadow, but once a year the whole village comes to life as for two days in April it plays host to 9000 people who come by coach and car from far afield to enjoy that harbinger of spring – a host of golden daffodils. They wander freely round the village, visit some of the older houses and many gardens both large and small and get an insight of what life is like in the country.

The villagers are busy weeks beforehand baking cakes and on the morning making sandwiches as all the teas are homemade. The

The Smithy at Thriplow

167

smithy on the green once again resounds to the clang of hammer on anvil and a succession of willing boys pump the bellows that make the sparks fly. Stalls set up on the green sell homemade produce, plants and of course daffodils. A local farmer clears his 15th century barn and 10 or so craftspeople demonstrate their skills – sheep shearing, spinning and weaving done by the village spinning club, willow baskets, wood turning, bargeware painting, pottery and lace making.

In the church the joyous splendour of springtime is enhanced by the massed blooms filling every nook and cranny and the soft music from the organ. A colourful display of embroidered kneelers greets the visitors. The project was started in 1980 by Lilian Turner, then secretary of Thriplow WI and over 80 kneelers have been made by the men and women of the village. Some depict scenes and houses in the village, some decorations from the painted ceiling in the church itself.

The Daffodil Weekend was started 20 years ago in a very small way to raise money for the church and the first year made £206. In 1988 the amount taken was over £10,000 and any village organisation can benefit with enough left over to give to a local charity every year. Not just the church but the school, playgroup, over 60s, cricket club, recreation ground and the village hall all benefit from the funds raised by the 400 inhabitants of the village.

Some years the daffodils are nearly over and some it is a job to find any in flower but always the weather is kind and visitors return year after year to sample the splendour of the daffodils and the friendliness of a small village working together.

Trumpington ✺

The shield with golden trumpets on the village sign is taken from the second oldest church brass in the country. This is the recumbent figure of crusader Sir Roger de Trumpington, 1289, in the parish church.

The village is now part of the city of Cambridge, but has many tangible links with its past. Traces of early settlements from the Iron Age and Roman periods on both sides of the river suggest that ancient trackways over the Gog Magog hills, from Essex and from the north west, converged at a point between Trumpington and Grantchester, with a ford over the river Cam. Byron's Pool is the site of the mill later made famous by Chaucer in his *Canterbury Tales*.

Trumpington has been relatively populous since medieval times. The base of the mid 15th century cross was found when the foundations for the War Memorial were dug in 1921 and it is now in the parish church under the tower. The village lock-up and pound were in the High Street, and the pillory post from the lock-up is now in the Cambridge Folk Museum. The last person to be locked up was in 1912, when a local policeman put in a man who was the worse for drink, to cool off. On unlocking the door the following day to take the man to court he was found to be in as bad a condition as the night before. It appears that his pals had kept him 'topped up' with beer administered through rubber tubing via the ventilator!

The tollgate keeper's house with weighbridge was sold in 1863 and converted into two cottages – now 'Weighbridge' and 'Tollbar' in the High Street. The remains of the weighbridge were found when the sewer was connected.

Whitelocks, a modern home for the elderly, stands in the High Street on the site of what was known as Whitelocks Yard. In 1724 George Whitelock willed his house to provide 34 poor households with coal, the coal to be of the cheapest! Coats and caps were also given annually to 18 poor people, the initials G.W. on them being a constant reminder to all of his generosity! Whitelock's house and malting were reconstructed in 1819 to be let as 20 cottages to poor people, and the land to be let as allotments.

Anstey Hall and Trumpington Hall probably occupy the sites of earlier manor houses. The government acquired Anstey Hall Farm in 1950 as the headquarters of the Plant Breeding Research Institute, but it has since been sold to public companies. Trumpington Hall has been in the Pemberton family since 1715. The Old House in Church Lane dates from the late 16th century, and has crow-stepped gables at each end and small windows with labels or hood moulds.

Trumpington had its witch in the mid 1800s, one commonly known as Mother Sivill, who was periodically hauled before the magistrates to be punished for her ill-doings. It also had Henry Fawcett, the blind Postmaster General, who died in 1884 and is buried in the churchyard. The Fawcett School in the village is named after him.

Tydd St Giles

As with most villages, Tydd St Giles is fairly quiet on the surface, but a great many inhabitants work hard behind the scenes to keep various activities going. The most spectacular of these is the annual Garden Fete and Flower Festival in June. The Flower Festival is staged in the beautiful church, which is 12th century and built of Barnack stone. It is one of three in the area with the tower standing apart from the main building. Recently money has been raised, within the village, to have the Great West Window repaired. This is thought to have been designed by Alan de Walsingham who also designed the Lantern Tower in Ely Cathedral.

The Garden Fete is held in the grounds of Tydd Manor. This is a fine house built during the 1600s and is set among lots of beautiful trees. The setting attracts a great many visitors to the fete, and proceeds from these have helped repair the church window.

There are several houses in the village about the same age as the Manor. One is supposed to have been the home of a smuggler. Another house about a mile away is called Hannath Hall after a previous owner. This man was something of an eccentric and when his wife died he refused to have her buried, and had food and water placed beside her coffin for three weeks. Could it be her ghost which is supposed to haunt the Hall?

Tydd St Giles is set right in the north east corner of Cambridgeshire and is, and always has been, engaged mainly in agriculture. Allied to agriculture in years past, Tydd had its own wheelwright and this man's daughter carried on the trade, after he died, virtually until her own demise. She is thought to have been the only lady wheelwright in the land. We also had a family of blacksmiths, two brothers, who were the last in a 200 year line of smiths. The last one died in 1983. With his death the blacksmith's shop disappeared.

Going back further in time the name of John Lumpkin can be found. He was the last of his family. When his father died John was left one shilling and he gave this shilling to some travelling players on condition that they danced over his father's grave. He once made a wagon inside a shed and had to demolish the shed to get the wagon out. His end came when he fell from a wagon in a drunken state and was run over!

Warboys ✦

Warboys is a typical fenland village, standing high on a ridge with extensive views towards Chatteris and beyond. It is in two distinct parts, the older near the church and former rectory, and the more recent along the High Street to the east and Mill End where the two windmills used to stand.

In recent years there has been a great deal of new building and the population has risen rapidly. There are a few very old buildings, notably the beautiful Manor House next to the church. It was built in the early 17th century and has Dutch style gables.

At the junction with the High Street stands the Clock Tower commemorating the Jubilee of Queen Victoria in 1887. This has recently been renovated.

We doubt whether she would be amused by the weather vane on top which depicts a witch on her broomstick. The story of the three witches of Warboys is well known, who were convicted of bewitching 14 individuals in 1593 and were condemned and executed but it is always thought to have been a trumped up charge.

Near the old Railway Station are Warboys Brickworks, but these are now closed. Their chimneys were visible as far away as Chatteris.

The church has one of the best broach spires in the county and was built in the 13th century. The chancel arch was Norman and various additions have been made over the years.

The name Warboys is interesting and is an example of a translation of a Saxon name into Norman–French. In the Domesday Book it is spelled Wardebusc which is thought to mean 'look-out wood'. This wood can even now be seen from seven miles away across the fens. The 'busc' part has been translated to the French 'bois' by the Normans and it was in the 17th century that the present name came about.

Present Warboys is a busy village with many thriving organisations and has four meeting halls, a large primary school, library, sports-field and social club.

Water Newton 🌿

This small village stands on the south bank of the river Nene between Alwalton and Stibbington. The A1 dual carriageway runs alongside the village, south to London and north to Stamford. The population is 66.

Water Newton was a Roman settlement called Durobrivae (the fort at the ford). Ermine Street, forerunner of the A1, linked London with the fortresses at Lincoln and York. To guard the point where Ermine Street crossed the river Nene, a small five acre fort was erected, probably to house an auxiliary garrison.

Pottery kilns where calcite-gritted cooking pots were produced have been found at Water Newton dating to the late 1st century AD. Clay and wood could be brought in by the Nene and the finished pots despatched by water.

A Christian silver hoard was found in February 1975, 27 silver objects and one gold. It is dated as not later than the 4th century AD. This new discovery is the earliest group of Christian religious silver from the whole Roman Empire and is a discovery of international importance. Before the discovery of the Water Newton treasure, the two earliest known Christian treasures were found in Italy and Turkey, both of the 6th century. Water Newton silver may now be seen in the British Museum.

The parish church of St Remigius stands close to the south bank of the river Nene. St Remigius was a Roman, the Bishop of Rheims 437–533 AD. His feast day is held on October 1st.

Three watermills at Water Newton are mentioned in the Domesday survey. The present mill, which replaced an older structure, bears the date 1791. It has been developed into five dwellings. Two old barns and farm buildings have also been made into homes in the last five years.

The manor house, now attached to the farm and the house near the Old Rectory gates, both 17th century, were once coaching inns, The George and Chequers, where large stables were attached. To the west of the village are old brickworks and about quarter of a mile south an old gravel pit.

Water Newton did have a village stores which closed in 1963. Now there are no facilities in the village. The village school closed in 1945.

Waterbeach 🌿

Waterbeach is situated five miles north east of Cambridge and 11 miles from the city of Ely. The village, then called Bechea, is mentioned in the Domesday Book when the population was about 335.

The name Waterbeach is derived from the Old English 'beche' meaning brook. In 1238 it was known as Waterbech. The names Landbeach and Waterbeach became established when the fens

Waterbeach village sign

became wetter and the higher ground in Landbeach became even more desirable. Stock could still graze in Landbeach when Waterbeach was flooded. In 1770 the historian, Rev. William Cole who had been curate at Waterbeach for three years moved to Milton. He wrote in his diary 'Not being a water rat I have left Waterbeach and moved to higher ground in Milton'.

If entering the village from the A10 by the Slap Up public house, one can see on the right hand side the remains of Car Dyke, an ancient canal built by the Romans which served as drainage, holding back seasonal flood waters, and probably was used for transporting grain as far north as Lincoln where there was a Roman garrison. The area has been marked by an inscribed stone erected by the Waterbeach Village Society in 1982.

Two abbeys exist within the parish boundaries – Waterbeach Abbey which is now little more than undulations in the fields to the south of the parish church, and Denny Abbey which was occupied at different times by the Benedictine monks, Knights Templar and the Franciscan Order of Minoresses (The Poor Clares). Now the Abbey is Crown property and a scheduled ancient monument.

The oldest building in Waterbeach is the parish church of St John the Evangelist. There are some surviving Norman features which indicate that its origins were late 12th century although in general the architecture is of the Early English and Perpendicular style. Much restoration and reconstruction has taken place over the centuries and is continuing in this century with the addition of a church room and new choir vestry. The bell and altar from the Fen Church, which was demolished after the floor collapsed during a harvest festival service in the 1960s, is in the south aisle.

Rev. Charles Haddon Spurgeon, the famous Baptist preacher was minister in Waterbeach during the 1850s when he was only 17. Later, he was invited back to lay the foundation stone of the present chapel which is named after him. It was built in 1863 when the dove house which the Baptists had been using was burnt down.

Another famous inhabitant of Waterbeach was John Denson who wrote *A Peasant's Voice* which gives a comprehensive picture of life in Waterbeach in the early 19th century. In 1823 he built his own cottage in Primrose Lane for £40. The cottage was demolished in 1952 but his great great great grand-daughter still lives in Primrose Lane.

The village green, surrounded by lime trees planted early this century, is the scene for the annual Feast Day which now takes place on a Saturday in the beginning of June.

There is a strong community spirit in Waterbeach. In 1970 the village school became a community primary school so that its facilities could be available to the residents of Waterbeach and neighbours, Chittering and Landbeach. In order to involve the whole community, the Waterbeach Community Association was formed in 1972.

Werrington 🐚

Werrington was an ancient settlement on the fringe of forest and fen. Of the several interpretations of the place-name, the most probable is 'the town of the Varini', a clan mentioned by Tacitus. Car Dyke, built by the Romans, still marks the eastern boundary of the parish. It is the only one of the surrounding hamlets to be included in the Domesday Book in 1086.

Until 1877 Werrington was in the parish of Paston. By an Order in Council of Queen Victoria dated 1853, the hamlets of Werrington and Walton were to form a separate parish on the death or retirement of the Rev. J. Pratt of Paston, which occurred in 1877. The parish church of St John the Baptist was formerly a chapel of ease to Paston until this time. The church consists of a nave with aisles and a porch, and a chancel with vestries on the north side. The oldest parts of the building date from the early 12th century. Restorations in the late 19th and early 20th centuries have left the building as it is today.

In 1929 Werrington was included in Peterborough city boundaries and a number of modern private housing areas were built during this period. Werrington has grown rapidly since that time, so that now there are three distinct neighbourhoods, each with its own shops, pub, school etc. These newer areas connect by footpaths, by cycle and by bus with the old village centre, now a conservation area and containing some attractive 17th century houses.

Werrington Feast, an ancient village tradition, took place on the first Sunday on or after 24th June, the Feast Day of St John the Baptist. This highlight of the village year is still celebrated as the Werrington Scout and Guide Carnival Saturday in June.

Werrington village through the ages has seen many changes. Through all these developments it has remained intact with a thriving social scene and a keen community spirit.

West Wratting 🌿

The village of West Wratting was probably founded in about AD 800 and it is thought that the name 'Wratting' came from the Saxon word 'wraett' which means 'The place where the cross-wort (a type of bed-straw) grows'. It is quite a small village (population 300–400) in the south of the county nestling against the Suffolk and Essex borders.

The Domesday Book mentions a church at West Wratting in 1086, probably built of wood. When the church of St Andrew was restored in 1730 it was found that an earlier church (believed to be Saxon) had stood on the same spot. Saxon foundations are within the walls of the nave, and a few pieces of Norman stonework are built into the present walls. The clergy and choir used to lead the congregation in a long crocodile through the village and allotments to bless the ground on Rogation Day. There is still a choir today and a restricted route.

The windmill is the oldest registered smock mill in England. This was probably built on the same spot as a former post mill and was last used for grinding corn in the 1920s.

The Hall is situated at the end of The Causeway next to the church. This is where Squire Frost lived and where he constructed a flying machine. This contraption was called an 'Ornithopta', and was built at the end of the 19th century costing £1,000 and taking nine years to complete. Local women were employed to stitch goose feathers on the covering of the framework to make the wings and it was powered by a 5 hp steam engine. A charge of a farthing was made to view the machine, which proved too heavy to fly. Hardly leaving the ground, it crashed nearby in a field of cattle!

The Second World War brought many changes to West Wratting. An aerodrome was built on The Common, Stirlings and Lancasters were among the bombers which flew on missions over Germany. There was also a searchlight battery nearby. Various army units were based either at The Hall (RAMC) or in tents in the meadow (RASC). Soldiers were always complaining about the plague of earwigs which tormented them at night. Members of the Eighth Army came to West Wratting on their return from North Africa. The Park House was used to billet toddlers evacuated from London. Most householders in the village took in evacuees. The three pubs in the village quickly sold out of beer with all the extra customers available! There were rumours that spies were operating from The Lamb – they supposedly had a radio transmitter, but one night they disappeared and nothing more was heard of them. Only one stick of bombs was dropped in the village throughout the war, missing all buildings and landing in the fields.

A folk myth inherited from Viking settlers may account for the tradition that the countryside between West Wratting and Balsham is haunted by the 'Shug Monkey'. The creature, either ghost or demon, is said to be jet black and shaggy haired with a monkey face and staring eyes. There is also a tale of 'The White Lady' who supposedly walks from Concordia House (on the common) to the woods surrounding the park.

Wicken ✤

Wicken is an attractive small village of about 700 people, including its hamlets of Padney and Upware. It has four village greens, a pretty pond, a pump, a war memorial and the remains of a market cross. At one end of the village is the 13th century church and at the other end is the Methodist chapel. In between are two general stores, one a post office, a garage, a hairdresser, a blacksmith, a pottery and a thatched pub. In fact several of the houses are thatched and those round the pond date back to the early 1600s.

There are two groups of almshouses. The benefactress Mary Hatch also started the old dame school and various charities, such as an annual contribution of 10 shillings worth of coal, half a crown for blankets and a yard of calico for the poor.

The Victorian Mission Hall is in the middle of the village and the centre of village life. It has been modernised and much improved inside and all the village has helped to raise money for it.

The church houses the tomb of Henry Cromwell, Lord Protector of Ireland and son of Oliver Cromwell. Henry lived a mile out of the village at Spinney Abbey, where the ghostly singing of the monks who inhabited the abbey long ago can still be heard on Easter Day. The monks used to walk to church along the main road, now the A1123.

Behind the church is Wicken Hall, a beautiful mellow building, the largest house in Wicken and it still retains traces of its original moat.

A main tourist attraction is Wicken Fen, haunt of birds, reeds, wild flowers and insects – especially insects! This is run by the National Trust who do guided tours in the summer months, followed by home-made tea, provided by the WI. On Wicken Fen is the recently opened longest board walk in the county, so disabled visitors and mothers with pushchairs are able to enjoy the peace and timeless beauty of the Fen. Wicken Fen can also claim to have the largest mosquitos in the country!

Wilburton

Evidence of early habitation has been found in the village and surrounding fens; flint axeheads, a hoard of bronze spears and swords, a gold Torque and Roman coins.

The village is on the high ridge of the Isle of Ely, much higher than the fenland. It is still an agricultural and fruit growing area but only a few people now work on the land. Most people find employment in Cambridge or Ely. There has been a decline in fruit growing and many acres of fruit trees have been pulled up and returned to arable crops.

The church is situated at the west end of the High Street. This dates from the 13th century. Opposite the church is the Rectory which is the home of the present Lord of the Manor, Mr B. S. Pell.

Bishop Alcock of Ely was Lord of the Manor 1486–1500. He entertained King Henry VII and the young Prince Henry when they came to visit the shrine of St Etheldreda at Ely. The Berristead, formerly the Manor House, is in Station Road and opposite the Recreation Ground. A new Manor House was built nearby in parkland, it is now a special school with day children and boarders from all over the county. Other houses of interest are Bell Gables, a late 17th century farm house of brick with curved gables near the church. Not far away is The Grange, a timber framed house, and The Tythe House in School Lane is another timbered house with a thatched roof. The Old School was built in 1855 and stands in a prominent position at the junction of School Lane and the High Street. It comprises a private house and the schoolroom which are now an antique shop and restoration workshop.

A new Primary School was built in 1958 at the far end of Carpond Lane, and currently has about 100 children attending it. The older children in the main go to Witchford Village College.

The Baptist Chapel is midway along the High Street. It has a large school room at the rear for extra meetings. Next to the chapel is the village hall let for all village activities and under the control of the Parish Council. At the rear of the Hall is a Social Club.

Before the War there were many shops and businesses, three public houses, garage, blacksmith, baker, hairdresser, butcher, grocer, post office and carpenter but now we only have the post office, one public house, two garages and a vegetable shop.

Many new houses have been built recently including two old people's groups of flats – Lucas Court and Bakery Close which is warden controlled.

Willingham ✤

The present village name is a contraction of Wivelingham, meaning 'the home of the people of Wifel'. This dates back to Anglo Saxon times so we believe that the village has been in continuous existence for more than a thousand years. It is one of the larger fen villages.

There are pieces of the original Saxon church in the present one. This is particularly beautiful with a wonderful angel roof and a wealth of wall paintings of great antiquity. Some of these have been restored and others are awaiting restoration.

The Isle of Ely is close and very clearly visible. Before the fens were drained in the 17th century, the Isle rising out of the mists with the cathedral 'the Ship of the Fens', must have been a dramatic sight.

Willingham people have always been fiercely independent. It has been said that at one time there was a problem fielding a cricket team as nobody would accept the captain's orders!

After the fens were drained mixed farming, with emphasis on cattle, was the main industry in Willingham despite occasional but devastating cattle plagues. Large scale fruit growing was established in the late 1800s when Chivers of Histon bought local fruit for jam making. The Kings of Willingham were Chivers' agents. Intensive growing of fruit and flowers on one acre could support a family, hence the number of Willingham houses standing on approximately one acre of land.

Willingham has always been a prosperous and hard working village. In the great days of horticulture the women worked hard with fruit and flowers, taking their children to the fields and orchards to play.

Horticultural crops are of course labour intensive and less labour is now available. Less fruit is grown but Willingham remains a farming village. Although it cannot be called an industry, Willingham can be proud of the beautiful prizewinning Percheron horses which are bred here.

There has been uninterrupted continuity of education in the village since 1593. The oldest school in the area was Willingham Subscription School. Unlike most of the early schools this was not endowed by an individual. There was a public subscription in the village, and sums from £20 to 3/4d were collected. The money was invested in land which accounted for the fact that a schoolmaster and one or two pupil teachers could always be maintained.

In 1856 the British School was opened. In 1902 all Church schools were taken over by the School Board. Nonconformists in the village (of whom there were a great number) decided that they did not want the Board School – they preferred their own. They 'passively resisted' paying the part of the rate set for education. Neither would they pay fines. In the end some of their goods were distrained and put up for auction. It happened that the auctioneer was in sympathy with the 'resisters'. He therefore not only gave his services free but the goods were 'knocked down' for surprisingly little money, and most of the 'resisters' bought each others goods!

Wimblington ✑

Situated between March and Doddington, Wimblington has a population of 1,400 and each year is expanding with new houses and council bungalows. This is a quiet village but certainly not a sleepy one.

In its early days, Wimblington consisted of a few small dwellings belonging to the lord of the manor of Doddington and before getting their own work done villagers had to do so much for him. Their work was concerned with animal husbandry, fishing, wild fowling, eel catching and repairing buildings. The main diet consisted of wild duck and fish, varied with seasonal lamb and mutton. Venison was a rarity imported from Huntingdonshire and Northamptonshire.

A great deal of building went on in Georgian times and some of the larger houses are still in use. The oldest house is actually 17th century (North House) and then there is a Georgian pedimented house (Addison House) a manor house and Hill House.

In 1809 a chapel was built in Chapel Lane and in 1850 another (Primitive Methodist) in Hook. These two served for several years but eventually a new one, built in 1877, became the only Methodist church. The parish church was consecrated in 1874 and by the end of the 1800s both churches had Sunday schools and choirs.

At this time the village had many tradesmen and was self sufficient – cobbler, carpenters, butcher, baker, grocer, greengrocer, milkman, blacksmith and dressmaker. There was a post office and cycle repair shop, an undertaker and Mr E. Bradshaw, a carpenter who made the coffins for people buried by the parish. There was always a lady to attend births and deaths, the best remembered being Granny Bradshaw and Mrs Cornish. Now we have lost most of these and the railway but there is still a post office, two general stores, a butcher and a newsagent.

This village is fortunate in having a very good school, in existence since 1802. It was an endowed school from the will of Mr Thomas Eaton, who wanted the village children to learn at least reading, writing and arithmetic. It was to be a mixed school of 40 boys and girls, girls leaving at 13 and boys at 14 years. Today it is a popular school where the children learn much more, but the fund from the original endowment buys many things they would otherwise not have.

The story of Wimblington would not be complete without a mention of 'The Park Carnation'. This was a hackney pony bred by his own stable from his prize winning stud by Mr W. Bellamy of Park House. This pony won every event it attended in the country and even swept the board at Olympia. It was so good to work and to look at that Bertram Mills wanted to buy it for his circus.

Wimpole 🌿

Wimpole is derived from 'Wina's pool'. Wina was a bondsman living near a pond or pool which was located near our only claim to fame – Wimpole Hall, now owned by the National Trust and giving new life to the village. Wimpole is only a small parish in size, 2468 acres with a population of approximately 200–300.

The original village of Old Wimpole and New Wimpole, built in 1845 by the 4th Earl of Hardwicke to house workers of the estate, are both closely connected with the Hall which in the past provided most of the employment. Now the National Trust provides a few jobs but most people commute to other villages eg cement works at Barrington and asbestos works at Whaddon.

A generation ago it was a thriving village with two public houses, a smithy and a church school attended by 80 children. The Hall, brickyard and woodyard gave employment. Wimpole and Arrington which also joins the estate had a cricket team. A shoe mender, John Reed, who was deaf and dumb walked four miles from Arrington every day to his shop in Wimpole especially built for him by Lord Clifden.

Now the village has two garages which must be a sign of the times and a small woodyard. The school was closed some years ago in the 1960s, the children going to a new school at Orwell.

The church of St Andrew is two miles from the village near the site of the original village next to the mansion house.

The Hall as it is today was built in 1632 by Sir Thomas Chicheley. Lord Radnor planted two miles of elms but these fell victim to Dutch elm disease. They have now been replanted by the National Trust. A later owner was Lord Harley, 2nd Earl of Oxford, after whom Harley Street and Oxford Street in London were named. The grounds were landscaped by Capability Brown, and in 1843 Queen Victoria and Prince Albert stayed there. Later owners were Lord Hardwicke and Viscount Clifden, whose son sold it to the last owners Captain and Mrs Bambridge – daughter of Rudyard Kipling.

From 1939 to 1945 the house was requisitioned and the army moved into the house and park. Now the National Trust house and farm attracts thousands of visitors each year.

Wistow 🌿

Wistow is a pretty village set in a valley with a brook running by, just off the Warboys to Ramsey road. It was an important village in Domesday times. Then it had a mill, church and brook.

The church is still part of the village but the rector is now shared among Warboys, Broughton, Bury and Wistow.

The village has a shop cum post office, one public house, The Three Horseshoes, a community bus service and a village hall. Children from the village are bussed to Upwood and Ramsey for school, but Wistow does have a thriving play group.

The Parish Council play an active role in the village and managed to provide a play area and 30 mph speed limits after lots of pressure from the WI. Farming is the main industry of the village.

Witchford 🌿

Witchford is a village on the A142 three miles west of Ely. Population at the 1981 census was 1208 and it is still expanding. In AD 607 St Augustine built a small church 'where the Wyche elm grows by the ford' and called it St Andrew's after his church in Rome. The present St Andrew's church dates from 1376.

The Baptist church is built on land given by Mr Cropley. In 1875 a foundation stone laying ceremony was performed when a copy of the Church Articles was placed under the stone.

In 1844 the Rev. Rackham gave the land on which to build a village school. Money was raised for this purpose and part of this school, together with modern extensions, makes up the present day primary school for about 170 children.

The village college stands on the site of a Second World War RAF camp. Building started in 1959 and has been extensively extended to cater for 700 students from 11 years to 16 years. This college is also used for adult education classes, sports etc.

St Andrew's Hall which was built in 1900 from money raised by the village community, stands on the site of the old village pound.

Facilities include a post office stores, village shop and two garages. Light industry in the village has recently been increased by the provision of a small Business Park.

Wittering 🌿

The village has been overtaken by the 20th century RAF Base and now only a few old cottages are left beside the outstanding Saxon church. The proportions are tall and narrow. There is distinctive Saxon long and short work and the massive chancel arch is most impressive. An aisle was added on the north side in later years and the tower and spire in the 14th century.

Woodhurst 🌿

The village is situated north of Huntingdon and St Ives, reached by a by-road between the A141 and B1010. It is 100 ft above sea level and is one of the best examples of a ring village surviving in England, practically unaltered in shape since it was first founded in thick woodland some 2,000 or more years ago. It was established along a trackway through forest, by widening the road at a convenient place both sides, forming an oblong space in which the village was built. The road was then divided when it entered the village to run round the perimeter until it came to the exit thus forming a ring around the houses and small fields it enclosed. At the entry and exit would be gates or some protection and along the outer edge of the encircling road would be a stockade to keep wild animals and would-be intruders out.

The church and manor house came centuries later and had to be built outside the ring as there was no room for them inside the ring fence. Other houses followed later. The ring road and the original shape is thus preserved.

During building in 1949 a number of skeletons and fragments of pottery of Saxon origin were found.

The oldest part of the church dates back to the 11th century and the building has many interesting features. The spire has a pepper-pot shape and we believe there is only one other like it in the country.

The village population at one time rose to 500 with seven public houses to serve them, but following two years of bad harvests it dwindled to 200 and remains near that figure.

In November 1834 a fire started in one of the farms and devastated almost half the village, leaving 12 families, all with children, homeless. It is reported that some of the village labourers appeared indifferent to the results of the blaze in as much as some were intoxicated and some engaged in pugilistic contests!

The custom of celebrating the festival of the church's patron saint – St John the Baptist – was revived in 1949 and is today expanded into a Feast Week sponsored by an energetic Village Hall Management Committee with a view to raising funds towards the upkeep of the village hall, having already achieved the building of the hall itself. They also arrange many other events in the village.

There is a charity in the village called Clay Pits Charity. Some fields are hired out to farmers and the money received is given to elderly folk in the village towards their coal or electricity bills each year. This was left by an elderly gentleman some years ago and is still continued.

Yaxley ✺

The village of Yaxley is reputed to be the largest village in England, which these days could be a disputed fact, for due to the large number of new housing estates plus factories that have been built in Yaxley, it now seems to be more a small township. However many of the old buildings in Main Street have been skilfully preserved and one is still able to find the peace and characteristic beauty of the old village.

Built on the edge of the fens, Yaxley has some of the most fertile land in the country. However at the opposite side of the village there are many seams of clay, which have been quarried and used in the making of bricks – hence the features of the boundary skylines are tall chimneys, which now are belching less smoke as the industry declines.

The history of wars is also written into Yaxley for the fens were used as a waterway to convey prisoners during the early 19th century Anglo-French wars. Flat-bottomed boats were landed at a point along Main Street and the prisoners marched up Church Street to their camp at Norman Cross. It appears that they found kindness in at least one person during their internment for a plaque is to be found in the church commemorating the life of an officer. The cost of this memorial had been borne by many prisoners out of their meagre pocket-money. During the Second

World War history was repeated when a prisoner of war camp was built in the village. This was mainly for Italian prisoners who were either put to work on the land or in the brick kilns. There was no plaque of commemoration for this period but many Italians stayed in the community after VE Day.

The largest part of Main Street contains listed buildings and on the small village green (where once the inhabitants held a market) one can still see the old village water pump and also an Edward VII pillar box, which is still in use.

At the present day there are three schools in the village for children up to the age of 11. In the Main Street of Yaxley there is a well equipped Fire Station which employs both permanent and retained firemen – it has grown to such an extent that it has its own social club on the premises. Besides an excellent Health Centre, Yaxley can boast a Senior Citizens' Retirement Centre (where a day centre for the elderly is also organised) and an adult Handicapped Home from where supervision is also given to five houses around the village where handicapped men and women make their home life.

The fens were drained in Cromwellian times by Vermuyden, and now we have beautiful views of acres of fertile crops stretching many miles to adjoining villages. These viewpoints are found on the hillsides leading up from the old village and also from bedroom and attic windows along Main Street. On a clear day it is a glorious sight!

Yelling ✎

At the beginning of this century there were about 58 families living in the village of Yelling. It was a thriving community with six farmers, a butcher, a cobbler, a pub, a school, a blacksmith, a vicar of our very own, a post office, a shop and a wheelwright and undertaker. The majority of cottages standing then housed several families in a terrace, but today they have been modernised and altered to provide a much more spacious home for one family. Most residents of the village then worked on the land.

Some new houses were built between the wars to replace some cottages which had fallen down. In 1930 the vicar died and the parish was taken over by the vicar of Graveley. Some of the craftsmen died or moved away in this period and were not replaced. No electricity was in the village then and fresh water arrived once a day in a lorry. You put out buckets for water at your gate: some days you got one bucketful, sometimes two!

After the Second World War another 14 houses were built, and electricity, piped water and the telephone were on their way. In the 1950s we still had a pub, post office, shop, butcher and school: though by then the school covered only the primary years and the older children were taken by bus the eight miles to Gamlingay.

By 1970 the only remaining amenity was the butcher's shop. The village school had finally closed but the building was bought for the village, to be a village hall and social centre.

Nineteen houses were built in the early 1970s, to bring the total village complement up to about 90 families. It is now rare to find employment in the village and residents commute in all directions. Farm boundaries have changed considerably, and of the six farmhouses only two now house a farming family. Our village vicar has had to become mobile to care for six parishes. In fact, everyone is mobile these days and we are visited by an occasional bus, the milkman, the library van and a butcher's van!

Index